T

7 ways for anyone to BOOST their income

7

ways for anyone to BOOST their income

How making a few simple changes
can significantly reduce your
outgoings and gain extra income

Anthony Vice

howtobooks

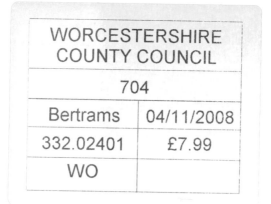
Published by How To Books Ltd,
Spring Hill House, Spring Hill Road,
Begbroke, Oxford OX 5 1RX, United Kingdom
Tel: (01865) 375794, Fax: (01865) 379162
info@howtobooks.co.uk
www.howtobooks.co.uk

How To Books greatly reduce the carbon footprint of their books by
sourcing their typesetting and printing in the UK.

British Library Cataloguing in Publication Data
A catalogue record for this book is available from the British Library

ISBN 978 1 84528 239 4

Cover design by Baseline Arts Ltd, Oxford
Produced for How To Books by Deer Park Productions, Tavistock
Typeset by Kestrel Data, Exeter, Devon
Printed and bound by Bell & Bain Ltd, Glasgow

NOTE: The material contained in this book is set out in good faith for
general guidance and no liability can be accepted for loss or expense
incurred as a result of relying in particular circumstances on statements
made in the book. Laws and regulations are complex and liable to change,
and readers should check the current position with the relevant authorities
before making personal arrangements.

Contents

Chapter 1

The First Way – Manage Your Bank Account

Many people will have started a bank account at college: when they start work, they have to manage a balancing act in order to handle their bank account most effectively.

There are two basic rules:
1. Do not overdraw beyond your agreed limit, and
2. Make sure that you have sufficient funds to meet direct debits and standing orders.

The reasons for these two basic rules are simple: if you do not obey them, you will have a lot of hassle, you may acquire a bad banking reputation and you will certainly pay – there are cash penalties for straying beyond what you agreed with your bank. Thanks to the internet, controlling your bank account is fast and easy; as an alternative, many banks operate a telephone service.

Making Your Money Work

Once you have your bank account under control, you face the other part of the balancing act: how to make your money work for you. You may have an interest-paying account, but you will quickly find that the rate of interest the bank pays you is far from generous. Your target for interest has to be that, allowing for tax, the rate you receive at least matches inflation.

The first answer is to set up a 'feeder' account: you agree with the bank that your basic account will be fixed at say £500 and that any excess will go into a savings account where you receive a higher rate of interest. Even that improved rate may not meet your target, so you put some money with one of the institutions named in the newspapers or on one of the internet comparison sites.

To make this set-up work, you have to keep a close watch on your bank accounts and be able to transfer money when a large payment arrives. You have to remember that it takes two or three working days to transfer a bank payment; you need to plan in advance if you go on holiday or if your job takes you away from home.

What Type of Account?

When you start to use a bank, your account will be in your name only. You may set up a joint account when you share a flat with friends; this becomes more likely when you marry or begin a relationship, particularly to handle household bills.

Example: How Safe Is Your Deposit?

Alan Dowding is especially relieved that protection is being improved for people's bank deposits. Alan, who lives in Newcastle, had £50,000 on deposit with Northern Rock, the local bank and mortgage lender which hit problems last summer – when the rules gave cover up to £31,700 on the first £35,000. (All the first £2,000, then 90% of the next £33,000.)

Alan has since learned that the answer, with a large deposit, is to spread it among several banks. His first thought was Halifax and Bank of Scotland, but his accountant pointed out that these form part of the same financial group, which could mean just one amount of compensation (depending how the companies are registered). From now on, Alan plans to make deposits jointly with his wife, so that they could both make claims – or divide the cash if they want to make separate deposits.

Two issues arise: a joint account is the responsibility of you both, so the bank will look to both of you to make good any shortfall. (What lawyers call 'joint and several' responsibility.) Secondly, you have to decide whether cheques on a joint account have to be signed by you both or just one of you. Both signatures means that you both know what is being paid out and in, though it can become cumbersome if one of you is away a good deal. Alternatively, you can have cheques signed by either one of you: in that case, one of you will not keep up-to-date – and if it ends in tears, one of you can clear the account.

You Need a Cushion

The first step in your banking arrangements should be to create a cushion to deal with the unexpected. This cushion should be equal to three to six months' income, and held in instant access accounts – which means that you can get hold of your money quickly and without any loss or penalty.

Nowadays, you should be able to get an interest rate which equals inflation after allowing for tax; this must be your objective when you are holding cash beyond the short term. Rates are widely quoted in the press and in search engines on the internet – you will probably find the best rates over the net.

You need to remember two things: one is that instant access does not quite mean what it says – to arrange a transfer of funds into your bank account will take a few days. The second important point you should not forget is that rates change: the bank or borrower which was top of everybody's list drops down and for reasons of its own it stops paying attractive rates in order to attract deposits. You need to watch the comparative tables and, if necessary, move your money – which, by definition, is not difficult, but *you* have to make it happen.

And you will have noticed if the appealing rates quoted include a bonus, for, say, six or twelve months; after that time the rate may fall quite sharply. This simply means making a note in your diary and telephoning at the right time: you may well find you can roll over your deposit at another attractive rate.

Called To Account?

You may be one of the several millions of bank customers whose account tipped into the red over the past six years and whose bank charged a fee – either for an unauthorised overdraft or because you exceeded an agreed overdraft limit. If you are one of these, read on with care, because in late 2007 the Government's Office of Fair Trading (OFT) dropped a large bomb in this particular pool.

Before the OFT intervened, the banks were charging what many people regarded as stiff penalties. The charges that were levied by some leading banks last year are set out in Table 1.1

Table 1.1: What You Had to Pay

BANK	UNAUTHORISED OVERDRAFT	FEES AND CHARGE
Barclays	27.5%	Paid item: £30 (Max 3 per month) * Bounced: £35 (Max 1 per day)
HSBC	18.3%	Unauth O/Draft up to £25 (Max 1 per day) * Paid item: £25 Bounced: £25 (Max 1 per day)
HBOS	29.8%	Paid item: £30 per day (Max £90 per month) Bounced: £39 (Max 3 per day)
NatWest	29.69%	Unauth O/Draft £38 Paid item: £30 Bounced: £38

*Not charged if first occurrence in six months (Source *The Times* early 2007)

This shows that HBOS (Halifax Bank of Scotland) charged for each bounced cheque or direct debit, with a maximum of three fees each day. It also charged a fee of £28 per month if you went over an agreed overdraft limit. (A paid item is charged when a cheque, direct debit or standing order is paid by the bank though there are not enough funds in the account.)

Many customers, spurred on by the press and consumer organisations, complained to their banks; by the time the OFT moved, several hundred million pounds had been handed back. This is how it was done:

First step: Write to the bank asking them for details of charges on unauthorised overdrafts over the previous six years. That information has to be provided under the Data Protection Act 1998 and the charge should be nominal. (Rules in Scotland are slightly different.)

Second step: Write to the bank explaining that you are a long-standing and loyal customer; you feel that the charges they have made for the unauthorised overdraft, or whatever, do not reflect the costs to the bank.

A reclaim is now off the menu, because of an agreement that no claims would go forward while the OFT's case was making its way through the courts: at the time of writing (2008) the process was expected to take at least a year: the High Court had to give its verdict, with the likelihood that the loser would take case to the House of Lords. But you need to remember how the claim procedure works, in the event that the banks win the argument – and if they do beat off the OFT, they may be tougher on any further claims.

Remember also that you can track back six years, as allowed by the statute of limitations. If you have all your records for that time, great. If not, it will probably make sense in any case to ask your bank to give you details of any fees and charges. If the banks win, you will need this information for your claim; if the OFT wins, you will need the information to get the compensation which could then become available. The key element remains the courts' final judgment and just how clear that proves to be. Nor is the issue as straightforward as it looks: some people argue that if big spenders go over their bank limits, that is exclusively their problem. Behind this argument is the prospect that, if the banks have to reduce charges for unauthorised overdrafts they will have to stop subsidising ordinary current accounts which, at present, are free.

You can see what could happen: if the courts, the government, the OFT, etc, feel sorry for people who paid these charges for unauthorised overdrafts and cut them back in future, that could spell the end of free banking for the rest of us.

Example: How To Move Money Abroad

If you want to move a large sum of money overseas, to buy a car or a property for example, it makes sense to use a foreign exchange broker. Some financial advisory firms also offer this service, which can save useful amounts.

For smaller sums, many people use their bank for a telegraphic transfer or to obtain an international banker's draft. There are alternatives, especially if speed is important: you can load someone's credit card or if you want to make a transfer there is the long-established Western Union and MoneyGram, which operates in the Post Office and Thomas Cook. You should expect to pay 5–10% extra for the cost of this service.

A modern electronic way to move money is to use PayPal, which offers competitive charges, though it may take up to a week for the funds to move from one bank account to the other. The sender and the person receiving both need to have an e-mail address and a free PayPal account.

So You Want To Borrow?

Most of us need access to extra finance from time to time. You may also look hard at the rates charged by motor insurers and others when you want to spread payments over a year, and decide that 10% plus is not for you.

For short-term borrowing, the choice lies essentially between credit cards and a loan. The chapter on credit cards contains a stiff warning from the chairman of Barclays on borrowing – but that refers to long-term borrowing, where credit card rates are extremely expensive.

The short guide to your choice is: use credit cards if you are switched-on in terms of financial management – good at keeping to limits and good at keeping to dates. Credit cards can be especially attractive if you can overpay for even a few months of the year.

The basic borrowing tool of credit cards has to be the 0% balance transfer, and/or the 0% on new purchases; and you will remember to cost in the 2.5–3% balance transfer fee. Some cards will allow you to avoid paying interest for 10–12 months, when you can go to another card (you need to take care on using cards for purchases when you make a balance transfer: see the chapter on credit cards). So long as you are skilled in handling the date of the balance transfers and in using the right card on fresh purchases, this method of borrowing is appealing.

Credit Card Extras

Compared with loans, credit cards also offer some potentially useful side benefits. Some will give you cash back, either as a cheque or a credit against your monthly account. Many credit cards offer free insurance cover on purchases; and all credit cards give you protection under the Consumer Credit Act.

The risks in credit cards are equally clear: if you don't pay off your balance in full each month you will be hit by a high interest rate. If you go over your agreed credit limit you will suffer a fee. And you should not use your credit card to withdraw cash – prefer your debit card.

Table 1:2 The Power of Compound Interest – How Long it Takes to Double Your Debt

BORROWING RATE	YEARS FOR DEBT TO DOUBLE
25%	3
20%	4
15%	5
10%	7

Why Not A Loan?

A bank loan looks to be the simple answer: there is nothing to compete with the credit cards' 0% balance transfers, but you can borrow a lump sum for up to 10 years and at a rate which compares favourably with those levied by credit cards.

Many loans charge a fixed rate, so repayment amounts should be consistent. This makes financial planning much easier – and you are in command of your repayment period. Setting up a loan is generally quick and simple.

Early Pay-Back Fee

The great drawback of a loan lies in its inflexibility. This appears when you want to pay back ahead of time: the majority of loans are repaid early, but this will probably bring an early settlement fee.

Two other points to watch for are the cost of payment protection insurance, which can be heavy, and precisely which percentage rate you are charged. The APR (annual percentage rate) may be less helpful than the TAR (total amount repayable) which will guide you on the cost of your loan. And the APR you have to pay may be increased if your credit rating leaves a little to be desired.

Raise Money On Your House

For people in the 30+ generation, the way to borrow medium term is through re-mortgaging. See Chapter 2 on Re-mortgaging, which has become a huge business and extremely popular.

Re-mortgaging is essentially a way of tapping into the rising value of your house and getting your hands on some of the 100% plus increase in its value which, on average, has taken place over the last ten years. Borrowing rates are much less than those charged by credit cards and generally lower than the rates on loans.

But re-mortgaging is probably not an option for the 50+ generation. Their mortgages will have only a few years to run, which means that re-mortgaging will be expensive. Even if there are a number of years left, a small mortgage also means that a re-mortgage may not make financial sense.

But for those of you 50+ there is another way to borrow on your house – and where you will not have to pay cash interest. We are living longer and the value of our houses grows steadily while living costs rise. Many thousands of people find their pension grows less adequate year by year, they need capital to buy a new car and to go on holiday, and their only major asset is the house they live in. This is why there has been a boom in equity release.

Two Ways To Equity Release

Older people in Britain are now raising between £1,500 and £2,000 million a year through equity release. The name says it all: you are tapping into the equity in your house, i.e. its value over and above any mortgage loan. Equity release schemes are operated by the major insurance companies and specialist advisers.

There are two types of equity release: the lifetime mortgage, which is the most popular, and a reversion plan, where you sell a part of the value of your house. You and your partner need to be at least 55 years old, and the terms will be better the older you are. In each case you get a lump sum, which is free of tax but which could affect your entitlement to tax and welfare benefits: you need to explore this issue before you commit. Both types of equity release are supervised by the Financial Services Authority.

No Monthly Interest To Pay

The lifetime mortgage works like a traditional-type mortgage, with one key difference – you do not pay out money by way of interest. You pay interest on what you borrow, but it rolls up until you and your partner both die or move into a care home. You should be offered the guarantee of 'no negative equity' – that the amount you owe will never exceed the value of your house, which is a useful defence against a possible drop in house prices.

You can see the appeal of a lifetime mortgage compared with an interest-only mortgage from a bank or insurance company: you have no cash flowing out, so you are free to use the mortgage money as you please.

Under a reversion plan, you sell part of your house – 100% if you choose – and you get a lifetime lease for your partner and yourself. The sale price, both for a reversion and a lifetime mortgage, will not be the market value of the house but a fraction, of between 25% and 40%. This is because the finance company is lending its money for an uncertain time (depending on how long you both live) which could be 20 or 30 years.

Who Is Eligible?

Most homes in England and Wales worth more than £75,000 or so will be eligible for equity release: some lenders stay out of Scotland, where the legal system is

Table 1.3: Lifetime Mortgages vs. Reversion Plans

	Lifetime Mortgage	Reversion Plan
How is cash released?	You receive a cash lump sum or income by taking out a loan, secured on your home. Interest rolls up on the loan until the end of the plan.	You sell a share of your home to the reversion provider in exchange for a lifetime lease and a cash lump sum.
How is the plan repaid?	When your house is sold, the loan plus interest is repaid out of the sale proceeds.	When your house is sold the reversion provider takes their share of the sale proceeds, according to the percentage share of your property that they own.
When does the plan end?	When the last remaining partner dies or moves into long-term care.	When the last remaining partner dies or moves into long-term care.
Can more funds be released later?	Top-ups can typically be arranged after a qualifying period. Or, you could opt for a plan where you draw down cash as and when you need it, only incurring interest on the amount drawn.	As long as you exchange less than a 100% share of your property, you can typically sell an additional share later if you want to generate extra cash.
What happens to inheritance?	This will be reduced but some plans allow you to guarantee an inheritance and most plans carry a 'no negative equity' guarantee so you will never owe more than the value of your home.	This will be reduced, but any share of your property that you retain can be left as an inheritance and you can also benefit from a 'no negative equity' guarantee.

different. If you live in a flat, the lease must be long enough to cover your life expectancy by a reasonable margin.

Some people have a mortgage when they decide to take out equity release – say the remainder of a 20- or 25-year loan. The equity release company will want this existing mortgage paid off, either before you sign up, or netted out as part of the overall transaction.

What Does It Cost?

If you take out an equity release plan, the important up-front fee will be for an independent valuation, which will form the basis on which the finance company lends you the money. You may also have an application fee and legal charges, which will probably be deducted from the lump sum; institutions vary in the help they will give you over costs.

One important difference between a lifetime mortgage and a reversion plan is that in the former case, you remain the owner of the house; under reversion, you are a lifetime tenant. You will be responsible for keeping your home in good shape and making sure that it is fully insured.

You can move house if you have taken equity release: you have to tell the lender and the new home will have to meet his requirements. Moving house will cost – the average cost of a move is now close to £10,000 – and if you change to a lower value property you may be asked to repay some of the money.

Taking On a Debt

Equity release is debt, secured on what is probably your biggest asset. This means that a lifetime mortgage or a reversion reduces the size of the estate you will leave to your heirs, so taking equity release should follow a family discussion.

The cheerful side of that coin is that your estate is reduced for inheritance tax (IHT), which attracts some people to equity release. You could take out a lifetime mortgage and distribute the proceeds, or some of them, among the family; if you live for seven years, those gifts will be free of IHT and the bill for your total estate will be that much less.

Living Longer Will Cost . . .

So what are the snags of equity release? The most obvious – from one standpoint – is that you take out a lifetime mortgage and live for another 20–30 years. This is very good for you, but the debt will have grown: if you took out a loan for £50,000, were charged interest at 6% and lived for another 25 years the debt would have reached just over £200,000.

The 'no negative equity' agreement will protect your estate, but the debt will make a hole in what you leave

Table 1:4: Fixed-Rate Lifetime Mortgage

AGE	MINIMUM PROPERTY VALUE £	MAXIMUM LOAN AS PROPORTION OF PROPERTY VALUE
60	88,250	17%
65	68,250	22%
70	55,750	27%
75	50,000	32%
80	50,000	37%
85	50,000	44%

Note: (a) In joint applications, maximum loan is based on the younger of the two ages (b) Minimum loan = £15,000

(Source: Norwich Union.)

to your heirs – unless house prices have been rising faster than the interest rate you have been charged. This underlines the case for a family talk before you commit.

Example
Jack and Jean Aspinall, now in their 80s – Jack is 84 and Jean 80 – find they need extra cash to redecorate the house and perhaps have a holiday. They choose a home reversion scheme rather than a lifetime mortgage as they want to leave 50% of their house to their daughter Elspeth.

Their house is valued at £210,000 and they are told they can expect to receive around £55,000 for a half-share. Jack paid the valuation fee upfront; he still has to find the legal costs, which he reckons will be about £350, and the application fee. This varies from plan to plan, but Jack is told he should expect to pay around £450.

. . . So Will A Change Of Mind

You should also appreciate that equity release is somewhat inflexible: lifetime mortgages are designed to last for the rest of your life or until you leave home to go into long-term care. If you want to repay early, you will probably be hit by an administration fee and an early repayment charge.

In the same way, you may be asked to take out a lifetime mortgage at a fixed rate of interest – which in a few years' time could look very clever or the exact opposite. On a fixed rate, you have the great advantage of certainty so you know exactly how much you, or your estate, will have to pay. As an alternative, you may be offered a rate of interest linked to retail prices with a cap limiting the maximum rate.

Age Helps

If you come to retire say age 65 and find your income is lagging and you need more cash, then equity release has considerable appeal – the main alternative is to generate capital by moving to a smaller home.

If you are in your 50s, it could make sense to take an interest-only mortgage for 10 years and then take out equity release: in this area, the older you are, the better the terms.

Summary

♦ Don't push your overdraft beyond the agreed limit; make sure there is enough money in your account to meet direct debits and standing orders. If you see problems coming, speak to the bank first.

♦ Think how you want to set up bank accounts. Look at a feeder account to get better rates of interest. Do you want a joint account – if so, who can sign it?

♦ Make sure you have a cushion of six months' income, available at a few days' notice, to deal with the unexpected. Go after interest rates which beat inflation after allowing for tax: check with the internet.

♦ Use credit cards to borrow through balance transfers – but you must be precise on timing and use other cards for purchases. If you like certainty, think about a bank loan, but certainty means a lack of flexibility.

♦ **If your house has risen in value, and you are over 60, think about equity release: lifetime mortgage or reversion. Under a lifetime mortgage, you don't have to pay out any interest – it rolls up, so if you live another 20 years or more the debt will show a big increase. Talk to the family before you decide.**

Chapter 2

The Second Way – Re-mortgage

Time To Re-Mortgage

Your mortgage will probably be the biggest debt of your life – and there is a good chance that it is costing you too much. If you are one of the borrowers, reckoned to be between one third and half of the total, who are paying the lender's standard variable rate, then you are almost certainly paying too much. The answer is to re-mortgage: that means moving your mortgage to another lender.

Myths have built up around re-mortgaging – that you can only re-mortgage when you move house, that you should stay with your original lender for the duration of the loan or that re-mortgaging involves a mass of complicated paperwork. These are just myths.

Example

Ted Lester has a £80,000 mortgage. He originally had a low-cost deal, but that has expired and he is now paying standard variable rate (SVR) of 7%. The SVR is the lender's standard rate, which moves broadly in line with the base rate that is set by the Bank of England.

Ted decides to re-mortgage with a deal at 4.8% for two years. He has an interest-only mortgage, for he believes that the future rise in house prices will enable him to pay off the mortgage when the time comes.

Under his original deal, Ted's monthly repayments amounted to £467. Under the re-mortgage, his repayments are now £320; he saves £147 a month, £1,764 a year and £3,528 over the two years of the deal.

Details of how you re-mortgage will be examined later in this chapter; there are costs, and for a few people a re-mortgage may not be worthwhile. But before you get there, you have to decide why you want to re-mortgage.

Saving Money

There is just a chance that you might not have to
change your mortgage. It's always worth asking your
lender to give you a new offer and move you to a lower
rate. The lender will want to keep your custom (he's
making money from the mortgage!), though most
lenders now reserve their attractive deals to tempt new
customers. If that is your lender's policy, you will have
to move to a different lender in order to save money.

Example: Re-mortgage To Pay School Fees

Keith and Jane Miller, who live in the
countryside, have decided to send their two sons
to boarding school. They know that finding the
fees out of income is going to be a struggle, so
they think about re-mortgaging. They have a
£100,000 interest-only mortgage on their house,
which is now worth £300,000.

They re-mortgage up to £200,000: half of this is
used to replace the existing mortgage. The other
£100,000 is set aside as a drawdown mortgage,
which Keith and Jane can call upon (and pay
interest on) when they choose – and this will be
used to help pay the school fees. If house prices
keep on rising, they might do the same again in
five years' time.

Raising Money

If you want to borrow to improve your house, or buy
a new car, you will soon realise that re-mortgaging is
a cheaper option than a personal loan or an overdraft.
The difference is potentially large: it can be several full
percentage points (several hundred basis points in the
jargon) which means that on, say, a £15,000 car you are
looking at a saving of around £500 a year.

To increase your mortgage you must have equity in
your house: equity is the difference between the value
of the house and the amount you have borrowed.
For many people, rising house prices have created
significant amounts of equity: the value of the house
has risen, while the mortgage has remained the same (if
it's interest-only) or even reduced (if it's on a repayment
basis).

Example

Peter and Joan Sims borrowed £90,000 to buy
their home five years ago. They took a repayment
mortgage – because Peter doesn't like taking risks
– and they have £79,500 left to pay. Interest is
6%, so that monthly repayments are £398.

The value of their house has increased to
£175,000, so there is equity in the property of
£95,500. They decide to make use of this equity
to pay £20,000 for a new car. Their joint salaries ▶

amount to £65,000, so on the traditional measure of 2.5 times, they could raise their mortgage to £162,500. Peter feels they should only go as far as £100,000, which would cover the cost of the car and still be under twice their joint income.

The Sims take out a new mortgage with a rate of 5.2% so that monthly repayments are £433. They realise that this is £35 more than they paid before – but if they had bought their car on a personal loan they could have paid much more!

Meeting an Endowment Shortfall

Several million homeowners have been sent letters telling them that their endowment schemes may not pay off their home loans. Buying a house on an endowment mortgage means making two sets of payments: (1) interest on the loan, and (2) premiums into an insurance endowment policy, which was meant to pay off the loan at the end of the 15 or 20–year life.

No less than six million people took out endowment mortgages. What went wrong was poor investment performance, so that insurance company bonuses were less than expected and the endowment policies fell short of the outstanding loan. A range of solutions have been tried: some people increased their insurance premiums (though many felt this was throwing good money after bad), some sold their endowment policies on the open market, while others took out repayment mortgages. Some, perhaps more enterprising, re-mortgaged to meet the shortfall.

Example

Ted and Jean Dodds have an interest-only mortgage of £70,000, with a rate of 6% and monthly repayments of £350. They have been making separate payments into an insurance company endowment policy that was meant to clear the loan at the end of the mortgage term.

But they have just received a letter warning them that there is likely to be a shortfall of £15,000 when the investment matures. So they remortgage to a home loan, which will reduce the mortgage balance by £15,000 by the end of the mortgage term. The endowment policy should clear the rest of the loan.

Alternative To a House Move

Some families even find that re-mortgaging is an economic way to raise money for an extension rather than moving house. Partly, this is a result of the heavy cost of stamp duty, which starts to bite over £125,000 and rises to 4% over £500,000 – where it would add £20,000 to the cost of the house.

Example

John and Harriet Brennan, who have two
children, feel that Harriet's mother should come
and stay with them rather than continuing to live
alone. They think about moving house, which
would mean paying stamp duty and removal costs
– plus all the hard work of changing suppliers,
credit cards and so on.

They have an interest-only mortgage of £250,000
on their house, which is now worth £350,000.
They pay interest at 6%, so that monthly
payments are £1,250. Their equity in the house is
£100,000.

They decide to re-mortgage and borrow an extra
£40,000 against this equity, which they can use to
add a granny flat. Their new loan carries a 4.8%
rate, so that monthly payments come slightly less
at £1,160.

John and Harriet do the sums: with the granny
flat, the house is now worth £400,000. To buy
a property of that value, allowing for all the
costs (stamp duty alone would be £12,000), they
believe they would need a mortgage of £350,000.
At 4.8% the monthly payments would be £1,400
– so they save £240 a month, and a lot of hassle,
by adding the granny flat rather than moving
house.

How To Re-mortgage: The Costs

There are costs involved in re-mortgaging. It is essential that you establish what these are, to make sure that at the end of the day you come out in credit.

Firstly, there are costs in leaving your present lender. If you re-mortgage during a fixed-rate or discount deal period, you will face an early repayment charge – which will tend to be higher the more recent the deal and could amount to six months' interest. If you took a cashback mortgage, you may face having to hand back some or even all of the cashback.

Even if you escape these charges, you will be hit by the administrative costs that the outgoing lender will make you pay. These can be called a deeds release fee or a discharge fee.

Secondly, the new lender is likely to want an arrangement fee – which he may be prepared to add to the amount of your loan. Early last year the Financial Services Authority clamped down on exit fees. But the bad news was that lenders began to put up arrangement fees – and the FSA confirmed that it would not take action if lenders put up interest rates or other charges.

Also significant are fees which do not go the lender but will be needed to make the switch. A valuation fee will be needed because the lender will want professional comfort that your property offers sufficient security.

Legal fees will also be needed on a re-mortgaging, though some lenders will pay for these – when you will have to use a solicitor approved by your lender.

When you have established all these costs, you need to work out your savings and outgoings over the next two, three and five years. You must be certain, before you commit yourself, that you will come out at the end of the day with a plus.

How To Re-mortgage: The Five Key Steps

The process of re-mortgaging comes down to five essential steps. You can carry out these yourself or use a mortgage broker. Unless you are especially knowledgeable, a broker is worth considering: their key advantage is that they survey the entire market, to get you the best deal possible. If you're worried about risk, residential mortgage brokers are regulated by the Financial Services Authority – so at least you will have someone to target if things go wrong.

1. Ask your lender for better terms. Get a redemption quote.
2. Choose your mortgage deal and get quotes from the new lender.
3. Work out the savings over two, three and five years, deduct the costs; decide if it is worth going ahead.
4. To go ahead, apply to the new lender.
5. Valuation, legal work – allow up to eight weeks to complete.

Example: Exit Fees – The FSA Moves In

The official watchdog, the Financial Services
Authority (FSA), threw the exit fee market into
confusion late last year. The one important point
to grasp is that you can reclaim an increase in
your exit fee if that takes place during the term
of your mortgage – from the time it is taken out
until the time it is paid off. The amount of the
exit administration fee will be spelled out in your
original mortgage agreement and that is all that
you should pay.

Many borrowers who redeemed a mortgage in
the last few years are likely to have a strong case
for a rebate. Even if you do not still have the
paperwork, go ahead and challenge your lender:
the industry is expecting to meet a heavy bill for
compensation!

You need to be aware of three other developments
which have obscured a pretty straightforward
picture. Some lenders reduced their exit fees for
new borrowers. A rather larger number re-named
exit fees, facing borrowers with charges such as
'mortgage account fees' payable at the end of the
mortgage term.

Lastly – to few people's surprise – some lenders
have responded by increasing both their exit fees

▶

and arrangement fees, which are usually larger. There are now wide differences among lenders' exit fees, from around £100 to about £300; arrangement fees can reach up to around 3% of the amount of the mortgage. A borrower may shop around, but finally has little option but to include these higher fees as part of his total mortgage cost.

People Who Should Not Re-Mortgage

If you had the skill, or luck, to arrange an excellent cashback mortgage or a heavily discounted deal, then almost certainly you should wait until it has completed before you re-mortgage. (In any case, you will probably face stiff penalties on a switch.) If your original deal was less than ideal – if your mortgage is surrounded by heavy redemption penalties – then you will probably also need to wait.

As you are looking for significant savings, it will not make sense to re-mortgage if your borrowing has been reduced by repayments – say to around £30,000–£40,000. Your benefits simply cannot be big enough to absorb the costs, and you may not find banks and building societies keen to lend at this level.

The same point applies if you are in the last few years of your mortgage; the costs of a switch are bound to be too large.

Which Type of Mortgage?

There is one key element still missing: before you commit to re-mortgage, you need to decide which type of mortgage you want. You may have been on a standard variable rate mortgage (SVR), as used by most borrowers – probably because you were transferred to this rate when your attractive special offer came to an end. Here are the options:

Standard Variable Rate (SVR)

This is the basic, straightforward, mortgage loan. The SVR is linked to the Bank of England base rate. As a rule, the SVR stands a couple of percentage points above base rate. Though SVR is linked to base rate, it does not follow every move: cynics suggest that SVR will go up when base rate does, but may not come down as much or as quickly. The appeal of an SVR mortgage lies in its simplicity. Its great drawback is that you, the borrower, are almost certainly paying more – maybe much more – than you need to. SVRs are widespread because many people are attracted by special offers from banks and building societies; these offers generally last for a specific time, and after that, you, the borrower, are switched to SVR.

Tracker Mortgage

The name says it all: your rate follows Bank of England base rate. You need to shop around – this is where a broker could help – because tracker rates can vary, from being rather below base rate to perhaps 1%

Mortgage ABC

APR: the annual percentage rate which the lender will charge you. This allows for the mortgage interest and related costs during the period of the loan.

ARRANGEMENT FEE: this is a once-only payment when you take out a new mortgage.

CAPITAL REPAYMENT MORTGAGE: this is the straight vanilla mortgage – you pay interest and the capital you have borrowed over a fixed period, normally 20–25 years.

CAPPED-RATE MORTGAGE: the interest rate you pay cannot go above a pre-agreed level. But often this rate is set high and you may pay higher interest than average.

CASHBACK: you get 5% or more of the mortgage back in cash, but you may pay higher interest – and have to hand the money back if you want to re-mortgage in the first few years.

DISCOUNTED MORTGAGE: you get a discount for the first two or three years, and then go on the lender's standard variable rate. (SVR below). There will be penalties if you want to re-mortgage during that period.

EXIT FEE: what you have to pay when you re-mortgage and move to a new lender.

FIXED-RATE MORTGAGE: the rate you pay is fixed for up to five years. You may or may not end up looking clever, but you will get certainty.

FLEXIBLE MORTGAGE: you can make underpayments or overpayments each month, rather than the same fixed amount – so especially useful for people who are self-employed.

INTEREST-ONLY MORTGAGE: your monthly payments cover just the interest on your loan, and do not repay any of the capital. Your cash flow will be better than on a traditional mortgage, and many people expect that rising house prices will eventually clear their debt.

PORTABLE MORTGAGE: can be transferred without extra cost to your new house or flat if you move within a pre-agreed time.

STANDARD VARIABLE RATE: this is the rate you will pay unless you have a discounted or fixed-rate deal – you should be able to save money by re-mortgaging.

TRACKER MORTGAGE: the interest rate you pay will move in line with the Bank of England's base rate, which is set by their Monetary Policy Committee.

higher. Some lenders also put in a 'collar', which sets a minimum below which your rate will not fall.

Many people are attracted to a tracker mortgage just because it is linked to an outside organisation: the rate is not fixed by the lender or even by a group of lenders. Your rate still depends on base rate, which also effectively determines SVR mortgages. One concern comes from people who worry about inflationary pressures in the UK. If these persist, you can expect base rate to keep moving upwards to contain price rises within the official guidelines. If you are concerned about future interest rates, there is the new prospect of interest rate insurance which could appeal to people with variable rate or tracker mortgages.

Interest Only Mortgages

In a traditional repayment mortgage, the money you hand over to the bank or building society goes two ways: (1) to pay interest on the loan, (2) to pay off the capital amount of the loan, i.e. the principal. In an interest-only mortgage there is no (2). You can see why interest-only mortgages are becoming more popular: the amount of cash you have to hand over is less, so you have more left in your pocket each month. The difference is significant: on a £250,000 mortgage, an interest-only deal could cost £400 a month less than a repayment mortgage.

But the difference in risk is also significant. When an interest-only deal comes to an end, you still have to find the money to pay back the lender. By contrast, your neighbour who had a repayment mortgage will then owe nothing.

Rising house prices have helped to make interest-only mortgages more appealing. People will tell you they are quite confident that in 10 or 15 years' time they will be able to pay off their borrowing by selling their house for far more than they paid for it, or by re-financing. And, they will say, they will have been building up their ISA tax-free investments, which can help reduce the capital debt.

With an interest-only mortgage you have more cash now, but you will have to pay back a hefty capital sum, whatever your situation, when the loan comes to an end. The choice is yours.

Discount Mortgages
These are lenders' short-term price cuts. You will be offered a discount, say of 1% or 2% for two or three years, off the lender's Standard Variable Rate or his Tracker Rate. When the discount period comes to an end, you will be switched back to the SVR or the tracker – which is when you will start to think about re-mortgaging. It may be possible to re-mortgage during the discount period, but it will almost certainly be too expensive.

Everyone likes a discount, and a price-cut of say 1% for three years is attractive. The key question in considering a discount mortgage is to establish precisely what is the discount from? Anyone can see that a discount of 1% on an SVR of 6% is the same as a discount of 2% on an SVR of 7%; you need to look carefully at the size of the discount and the length of time it is available, and you may find it useful to employ a broker. No one went bust by taking a discount.

Fixed Rate Mortgages

On fixed rate mortgages, the rate you pay is fixed for an agreed period, which will generally be for three or five years. You may be able, if you choose, to fix your rate for longer but that will prove costly.

If what matters to you is the amount of cash you pay, then you do not enter into a fixed-rate deal when interest rates have been rising and base rate may be close to its peak – as looked likely in the later months of 2007. By common sense, the time to go for a fixed-rate deal is when interest rates are low.

But there is more to fixed-rate deals than making, or not losing, money. You are getting certainty and that in itself is something of value. The point is not theoretical: if your mortgage payments are only just affordable, you simply cannot afford to take a view on interest rates. You need to keep your mortgage interest costs under firm control and the only way to achieve that is through a fixed-rate deal. You could even split your mortgage between a fixed-rate deal and a tracker, preferably for the same term. This may look cumbersome, but represents about as good protection as you will get.

Fancy a 25-year Mortgage?

Earlier this year, the Government announced plans to promote long-term fixed-interest mortgages – which are already available from some banks and building societies. Rates are fixed slightly higher than for a two or five year fixed-rate; so far, not many people have rushed to fix their borrowing costs for the next quarter-century.

Existing long-term mortgages typically offer some limited ability to overpay but there will be penalties for redemption, at least for the initial 10-15 years. Many people still seem to believe that house prices will rise long-term, so they will be able to re-mortgage on better terms.

Capped Mortgages

'Collars' and 'Caps' are two pieces of jargon that have recently hit the mortgage market: they simply stand for 'minimum' and 'maximum'. Lenders might want to put a collar in a mortgage agreement, say in a tracker mortgage. A cap, by contrast, is of interest to you the borrower.

The rate you pay on your loan will move in line with base rate, but the cap will set a maximum above which your rate cannot go. You are therefore protected against a surge in interest rates. If that is your concern, then a cap will appeal to you. But be aware that it does not come free: you may find that the cap is set high and you may also find that your starting rate is somewhat higher. As in so many financial cases, you get what you pay for; you have to decide where your priorities lie.

Cashback Mortgages

The name says it: when you take out your mortgage the lender hands over cash equal to 5% or perhaps 10% of the amount you have borrowed. This cash can be very useful, especially when you are moving house or if you are a first-time buyer. But, as ever, you have to pay for the happy ability to pocket a lump of cash. You are likely to pay in two ways: you will probably find that your cashback mortgage charges you a higher rate than a standard arrangement. You will also find that you face early repayment charges if you want to pay back your loan within a fixed period, generally five years. This is why re-mortgaging is expensive for people who have recently taken out a cashback mortgage.

Offset Mortgages

Offset mortgages are one of the more recent, and sophisticated, arrivals. They are attractive to people who have built up some savings and they are tax-efficient: they will especially appeal to higher-rate taxpayers.

These mortgages allow borrowers to use their savings and current account to offset the cost of their home loan. So, instead of receiving interest on their savings and current account, borrowers save on the interest they pay the lender.

This has two great advantages: (1) the interest you receive on a savings account is less than the rate you pay on your mortgage, and (2) you would have to pay tax on the interest you received: far better to pay less interest on your loan rather than earn a lower rate of taxable interest on your savings.

You will probably pay a rather higher rate than on a traditional-type mortgage, and you will probably need to have savings of at least £25,000 for the deal to make sense. For people who have built up that amount of savings, and who pay higher-rate tax, offset mortgages can be very appealing.

Example

Arthur and Joan Halliday take a £200,000 offset mortgage on their £250,000 house. This costs them about £80 a month more than the prevailing best fixed-rate home loan deal, but Arthur and Joan have savings of just over £20,000 and can put £4,000 a month into their current account with the lender.

They calculate that they will save more than
£50,000 in interest over the life of the loan – and
that they will be able to repay the loan itself more
than four years early.

Extending Your Mortgage Term

This is included primarily as something which you
should avoid – or treat as a decision of last resort. The
appeal is clear: if you want to cut the cost of monthly
repayments, you can extend your loan term. The
downside is that you pay interest for a longer period
and this will add to the total cost.

Example

Ted and Rose Brooks have a £200,000 loan over
25 years at 5%. Ted is between jobs, so they are
anxious to cut back on their monthly outgoings.
They find that if they extend the loan by five
years, to 30 years, their monthly repayments will
fall from £1,169 to £1,073 which will save them
more than £1,000 a year.

The snag is that they will be paying interest for an
extra five years, which pushes up the cost. On the
original 25-year deal they would repay £350,000.
Adding the extra five years will increase their bill
by around £36,000, or more than 10%. It would
be cheaper to take out a bank loan or arrange an
overdraft.

Don't Stop Re-Mortgaging!

Many thousands of people have re-mortgaged – some of them more than once. Re-mortgaging is a straightforward financial operation, which you should continue to put into action so long and so often as it makes financial sense.

In a year's time, the best buy which you just achieved could have fallen far down the ratings. And if you have chosen a deal which covers a specific period, say two or three years, you should start planning your next move a few months before the deadline.

If you want to keep saving, you have to keep active!

Summary
- **Re-mortgage if you are paying the lender's Standard Variable Rate – you could save significant amounts of money.**

- **Re-mortgage if you have equity in your house (equity = value of the house minus any borrowings) as a cheap way to buy a new car or build a new kitchen.**

- **You need to do the sums before you commit: you will have fees from the lender you are leaving and other fees from the one you are joining. You will also have charges for valuation and legal costs.**

- This means you should not re-mortgage if your mortgage is small (under £50,000) or has only a few years to run. You will not be able to make sufficient savings to outweigh the costs.

- If you are one of the millions who took out an endowment mortgage that is not performing, think about re-mortgaging as an alternative to, for example, selling on the market.

- Think carefully, maybe speak to a broker, about the different types of mortgages which are now available: capped and collared, discount, fixed-rate, tracker. Remember that you will pay for what you get – and if you decide to take out a fixed-rate mortgage, resolve never to look back!

- Don't stop re-mortgaging: do so just as often as it makes financial sense.

Chapter 3

The Third Way – Sort Out Your Credit Cards

Credit Cards: The Dos and Don'ts

Matt Barrett, chief executive and then chairman of Barclays Bank, said it all. He was asked by a House of Commons select committee whether he used any of the Barclaycard products. He replied that they were much too expensive for him. Credit cards offer convenience and some important financial and legal advantages; but they become expensive if you stray outside the fixed paths.

The first step is to sort out the cards in your wallet. These can be debit cards, charge cards or credit cards.

- Debit card is the simplest: it moves money from your account to someone else's. A debit card is in effect a plastic cheque, but which works much faster. Many people use debit cards because they are simple and convenient.

- Charge card – probably the best known is American Express – requires you to pay all that you owe by the date specified. You cannot carry the debt over, i.e. there is no credit element; this amounts to the same as a credit card (except from a legal standpoint) where people pay off all the debt by the due date.

- Credit card, such as Visa or Mastercard, where you get your monthly bill statement maybe two or three weeks after your purchases. You must make a minimum payment, perhaps only 5% or less of the total, or you can pay off the total amount. If you run the debt on, you will pay an annual rate anywhere between 10% and 20%; that is what Matt Barrett meant – if you borrow at 20% your debt will double in only four years.

Paying On Time

You need to avoid doing two things which credit card companies dislike and for which they will charge you – paying late and spending more than your limit. The way to be sure to pay on time is simple: set up a direct debit with your bank, to pay off all the debt, or the minimum or perhaps a fixed amount. Sending a cheque will take time and some credit card companies will not accept post-dated cheques. You could telephone and use a debit card, but a direct debit is safe and much more convenient.

Keeping within your credit limit can be more difficult, because you cannot be certain when the supplier will bill the credit card company; if they take their time, your monthly bill may include payments that go back several weeks. The solution is to keep a running check on the state of your balance, either by telephone or more easily over the internet. This is worth doing on a regular basis, partly to avoid the charges but also because a record of over-spent limits could affect your credit record. (Some credit card companies will e-mail you when you get close to your limit.)

Go and Buy – at 0% Interest

Credit cards offer two great financial advantages which you should exploit. These are nil-interest purchases and nil-interest balance transfers. (Note: The terms of both types of deal can change quickly, so before you commit you should check through the internet or the press.)

On purchases, the deal could not be much simpler: you apply for the card (some deals are open only to new cardholders) and for up to 12 months you pay no interest on what you buy. Your debt just rolls forward to the end of the interest-free period – provided always that you do not breach the credit limit which the card company has given you.

Financially, the appeal is clear. If your purchases total £500 a month and you pay no interest for six months, you have been given an interest-free loan averaging £1,500. That represents a significant financial benefit.

Each month, you will have to pay the minimum which the card company lays down. This varies among credit cards and could be between 2% and 5% a month: in that case, you will have paid off part of your debt by the end of the interest-free period. When that period comes to an end, you will have a large amount to hand over – one company will even send you a text alert five days before the payment is due.

You need to plan ahead how you will pay the rolled-up debt. If you run it on, your interest rate will rocket from zero to a high figure. If paying it off gives you problems, you need to talk to your bank about a loan or overdraft. Alternatively, you could arrange a 0% balance transfer with a new credit card – as discussed in the next section. Borrowing on your credit card, always remember, is expensive.

Transfer Your Debt – at 0% Interest

If you have built up debt on a credit card, then a 0% balance transfer could be just what you need. Deals change, and here again you need to check the up-to-date data before you go ahead.

Balance transfer means just what it says: if you have a debt on a card, you can transfer this debt to a new card and pay no interest for the pre-arranged period.

Example

Alan Connolly owes £5,500 on his ABC credit
card, which is costing him 14% or £64 a month.

The XYZ credit card offers Alan a 0% balance
transfer for 10 months. There is a 2% fee, which
costs him £110 – but over the 10 months Alan
will have saved £530. This is an easy decision to
make!

He reckons that at the end of the 10-month
period he may be able to pay off the £5,500, and
there is always the chance that he will be able to
make another low-cost balance transfer.

There is one point to watch: if you make a balance
transfer, you should not use your new card to make
purchases. Many card companies will use the payments
they receive from you to pay off the lower rate debt
first, leaving you to pay higher rates on what you buy.
The simplest answer is to use another card.

Cover From Your Credit Card

Probably the biggest single benefit from your credit
card is that it will cover you when you buy something
which does not work or where the supplier goes bust;
and the courts have now decided that the protection
extends abroad as well as in the UK. This cover arises
from the Consumer Credit Act 1974 and applies to

goods and services which at present cost from £100 up to £30,000. (Charge cards and debit cards are not covered – the credit element is the key.)

Example: Credit Card Protection

Joan and Darren Coxon see a sofa they like. It costs £600, and the salesman tells them it will be delivered in four weeks; he needs a 10% deposit so Darren pays £60 on his Visa card.

Four weeks pass, but no sign of the sofa. Joan phones the salesman but can't get through; she goes round to the shop but she finds it is closed with a notice 'Ceased Trading'. The company has gone bust.

An adviser tells Joan and Darren that they are unsecured creditors; in the real world, their chances of getting their money back are virtually nil. But he also tells them that they can claim against the credit card company – under the law, it is responsible along with the retailer for any breach of contract and/or misrepresentation.

Darren points out that his deposit was less than £100, but the adviser explains that what matters is the cash price. Joan and Darren recover their £60.

Loyalty Cards

Major retail groups, such as Tesco and Marks & Spencer, issue credit cards that give you bonus points when you shop there. The bonus points represent a small percentage of your spend – and an even smaller percentage if you use the card elsewhere.

Every three months or so the retailer will send you a voucher depending on the number of points you have built up. The voucher can be used only to buy goods in the store; the aim of loyalty cards is to build turnover.

Store Cards

Store cards are issued by department stores and usually can be used only in that group. Their objective is the same as loyalty cards – increase the shop's sales – but they do not send out vouchers. Instead, cardholders are often offered a discount on initial purchases when they take out the card and privileges such as extra discounts on sales or being able to access sales a day early.

Store cards share one potentially hurtful feature – their interest charges are higher than those of the credit card companies. Loyalty cards tend to charge rather above average, but store cards charge in the 25–30% range, which will double your debt in three years or less.

Use store cards for the useful benefits they bring in a store you patronise, but make sure that you pay your debt by the due date and avoid having to pay for credit.

Cashback Cards

Some people pay off their credit card bills by the due date and never use credit. For them, balance transfers are of no interest; 0% on purchases for a period can appeal, but there is a more direct method – get back a percentage of what they spend.

Cashback deals have become less widespread and less generous than a few years ago, but there are still a number of cards which will hand back cash on an ongoing basis of 0.5% or 1% and even up to 1.5%. These payments will come annually either as a credit on your bill or as a cheque, generally with a limit on the amount of purchases for which you can claim. Other cards will give you air miles or points which you can spend for holidays, cinema tickets, etc.

If you are one of the significant minority who pay their bill in full every month and do not use credit, then cashback deals and/or interest-free purchases can give you a benefit of several hundred pounds a year. You should use your card as often as possible, as opposed to cash, even for small purchases.

Watch out also for cashback offers to new customers: one card company was offering 4% cashback for the first three months and 1% after that. If you spent £8,000 evenly over a year, you would collect a handy £140 cash at the end of the 12 months.

Credit Card Cheques

Some credit card companies will send you cheques
which you can use on your credit card. You will be told
that you can use the cheques up to your credit card
limit and pay them off over time. Ignore these offers.

You may be charged a handling fee for the cheque.
Even if you escape that, you should appreciate that
credit-card cheques are treated as cash advances, which
may involve a fee, while interest will accrue as soon as
the cheque is cashed. This means that even if you pay
off your bill in full you will be charged a full month's
interest on the amount of the cheque. And you will not
be covered by the Consumer Credit Act for anything
you buy using these cheques.

Using Your Card Abroad

Many countries accept credit cards nowadays, especially
in Europe and the US – where you may be offered a
discount if you pay cash! When you use your card, the
important point you should take on board is the foreign
exchange fee, typically 2.75%. If you have an £800
hotel bill, this will cost you an extra £22.

Just a few credit card companies do not charge this
fee: Nationwide is one of the leading companies which
waive, while Saga (catering for the over 50s), waives
the fee in Europe and charges only 1% in the rest of the
world.

You will also face this foreign exchange fee when you draw cash abroad. You should use a debit card rather than your credit card to draw currency from an ATM, where you will pay a withdrawal fee of 1–2% often with a cash minimum of £1.50–£5. But even when you use a debit card (unless it's from a company which does not charge), you will suffer the foreign exchange add-on.

Travellers' Cheque Card

Taking money overseas can be a problem: cash is risky, while travellers' cheques suffer heavy commission in many countries when you cash them at the bank.

To meet this problem, some companies have devised the loaded card, i.e. a prepaid credit/debit card. You buy a card in the UK, load it with dollars or euros and then use the card abroad to make purchases or to draw cash. There are costs: when you buy the card, when you draw cash abroad, while your own money sits in the card not earning any interest.

For some people, the prepaid card has appeal. You can determine in advance what you are going to spend; if your son or daughter, backpacking in Australia, runs out of cash you, still in the UK, can re-load their card, often over the telephone by using your own credit or debit card.

Example: Costs Of A Prepaid Card

Brian Sellers' neighbour gave his son a prepaid card to travel abroad in his gap year. That worked well, so Brian gets one when he and his wife go to Benidorm. Brian finds the card convenient but costly compared with using an ATM. He has to buy the card to start with, and there is a fee each time he draws cash in Spain. There is no foreign exchange cost, but when Brian gets back to England and returns the card, he finds there is a fee on redemption.

But If You Lose Your Card?

All of us keep a close watch on the plastic in a wallet or handbag. Credit card companies will tell you about card protection agencies with which you can register your cards and tell them if your cards are stolen.

The basic rule is simple: tell the card issuer as soon as possible. If you can report the loss before the thief has time to use the card, then you have no liability for the extra items which appear on your credit card bill. In any case, under law you are only liable for £50 spent by the thief, unless the card company can show that you acted without reasonable care.

Chip And Pin

Chip and PIN were introduced to combat credit card fraud because the chip cannot be 'cloned' – which happens when fraudsters copy data from the magnetic strip on your card. Fraud in this country has been reduced, but enterprising crooks have taken to using British cards which they have cloned in overseas markets, where controls are less rigorous.

The basic anti-fraud advice is never to let your credit card out of your sight – which means not leaving it behind the bar at a pub when you are paying for drinks. Two other steps will help: keep your PIN secret and choose a number that someone else would find it hard to guess. Your claim for compensation will be rejected if you did not take 'reasonable care' to protect your PIN and some banks are arguing that customers could have protected their PINs better by choosing less accessible numbers. (Remember: your birthday is on public record.)

The second choice you can make is to use cash at riskier sites – for example, a petrol station which you do not visit often. It also makes sense in that situation to use a credit card rather than a debit card: if the crooks get your debit card details they can access your direct debits and your entire bank account.

And If You Lose Your Card?

Remember: all a thief needs is your card number, the card expiry date and your billing address. Armed with these data, he can order goods over the phone or on the internet and you won't even know, as your credit card sits safely in your wallet. The thief has stolen your identity – one of the fastest-growing crimes in the UK today.

The thief may have bought your data from a shop assistant or a waiter in a restaurant where you used your card. But by far his most likely source is you yourself. In your paper rubbish he can find what he needs – not just from a credit card bill but from a utility bill or even a business letter. You have to destroy this evidence effectively using a shredder or simply spend time with a pair of scissors.

Getting your identity back can be tedious and time-consuming – a good case for protecting it in the first place. But the serious threat is the liability for what the thief has spent. You have two lines of defence if the card issuer turns to you:

1. You can show that you held your cards all the time, giving the presumption that any transactions were not authorised and so not your responsibility, and
2. You can show that under the rules of the voluntary Banking Code you acted with reasonable care.

The defence of 'reasonable care' has appeal, because it is up to the credit card company to show that you were careless. But there are worries: if you just put all your credit card and other bills in the rubbish the thief will have an easy job. The formal advice is that you should dispose of your credit card receipts 'carefully'. There is a warning here: if you act without reasonable care and this causes losses, then you may be responsible. The moral has to be: shred or cut up all your personal financial papers.

The One Action To Avoid

Credit cards offer immense convenience and many advantages, which explains why around 75 million are now in circulation. But the one thing you should not do is borrow long term on your credit card: while borrowing is very easy, the cost is high, as Matt Barrett of Barclays pointed out: at the interest rates they charge, your debt will double in only a few years.

This warning is not meant to exclude the occasional unexpected dip into the red. What is at issue is a significant level of medium- or longer-term borrowing. If that forms part of your financial requirement, then you should go to your bank and arrange an overdraft or a personal loan, for which you will pay half or less of the credit card rate.

Or you can arrange a low-cost balance transfer, which will at least buy you up to a year's breathing space. And if you are looking to pay off credit card debts along with other amounts you owe, there are the options of re-mortgaging or equity release.

Example: How £100 Compounds

RATE%	AFTER 3 YEARS	AFTER 5 YEARS
18	£164	£228
20	£172	£248
22	£181	£270
25	£195	£305

Summary

♦ **Two golden rules – pay on time and stay within your spending limit. Otherwise, it will cost you!**

♦ **If you always pay off your bills, think about 0% purchase offers – but you will have to pay the card minimum each month and stay within your spending limit.**

♦ **Balance transfers at 0% are an attractive way of borrowing. Cost in the transfer fee; will you pay off at the end of the deal or do you hope to keep rolling over?**

♦ **Credit cards give you protection under the law if your supplier goes bust. This also applies abroad – charge cards and credit card cheques excluded.**

♦ **Pay off store cards in full: in general, their interest rates are relatively high.**

- Choose your card when you go abroad: if you want to avoid a foreign currency charge, think Nationwide, Post Office or Saga in the EU.

- Loaded cards can be useful if you want to set a budget or if you have a backpacking son/daughter. But allow for the operating costs.

- ALWAYS shred or cut up your bills and statements and any letters which refer to your financial situation.

Chapter 4

The Fourth Way – Keep Your Tax Bill Down

Are You Paying Too Much Income Tax?

According to the official National Audit Office, several million people may have overpaid their tax because of deficiencies in the pay-as-you-earn (PAYE) tax system. The tax system has become complex, which means that it can be prone to errors -with a number of key points for likely mistakes, such as when people move from basic to higher-rate tax.

So what do you do? You could go to an accountant, for which you will pay. Many people, whose tax affairs are fairly straightforward, will handle their own tax direct with the Revenue. For both sets of taxpayers, there are a number of basic rules to follow – even if you decide to go to an accountant, he will depend on you for full and accurate information.

Tell the Revenue

Your first step has to be to tell the Revenue all they need to know about you and your family. This means your date of birth, your marital status, where you live, what work you do, your National Insurance Number – and the same, if it applies, for your partner and your children.

The next thing you have to resolve is to keep records, and keep them for at least six years. You have a legal responsibility over record-keeping; just as important, you will need these records if you get into a dispute with the Revenue or when they make a mistake. Remember that they are not infallible, and you may be the unlucky one who suffers.

Read What They Send You

For the same reasons, you should read with great care whatever documents you receive from the Revenue. You should get an annual coding notice early in the year and you can expect them to send you assessments. Pay particular attention if the Revenue changes the District which handles your tax affairs: this is done for reasons of internal staffing and organisation, but there are obvious possibilities for error if your files are moved from say, Leicester to Cornwall.

Your coding notice is a must for you to read and check. This shows all the allowances and deductions to which you are entitled and this information is used to work out your tax code. Pay close attention to your coding notice when you reach age 65 and 75 when your allowances increase, subject to your income.

People who have had changes to their working lives are reckoned most likely to be paying the wrong amount. You could, for example, be put in an emergency tax bracket if you failed to hand in your P45 when you changed jobs. If you had a company car but no longer have one, you should check that your code reflects your current situation.

When you read what the Revenue send you, be on the alert for any deadlines. It is a very bad idea to be late – especially with your tax return itself. You will have to pay if you are late and your file will start to suggest that you are either careless or being slow for your own financial advantage. That is not something which you want to encourage.

The Key Tax Forms

P45: you are issued with this form when you leave your job. It's important to keep this and give it to your new employer – otherwise you may be taxed too much.

P60: this is the summary you should get, usually every May, which sets out the amount you were paid and the tax deducted during the previous financial year. Keep this and check it against the Revenue's figures. (You get a P60U if you are unemployed.)

P11D: this normally arrives in May or June and shows the taxable benefits you received from your employer over the previous tax year – including your company car. Check this form, which the Revenue will use to add up your tax bill, especially for instance if you changed your car during the year.

On timing, you need to be aware that from the 2007–8 financial year the Revenue is cutting three months off the period in which you are allowed to file a paper self-assessment return. This must now reach the Revenue by 31 October – only about six months from the end of the financial year – though you still have to 31 January to file a return online.

Your Family Tax

You are now a late twenty/thirtysomething with a partner and two small children. Your first step is to make sure that you both are getting your proper tax allowances. If you work for an employer, you can simply go to the salaries department. If you are self-employed, you will have to work it out yourself: log on to the internet or buy one of the paperback tax guides which are published every year, such as the *Daily Mail Tax Guide*.

More fundamentally, you need to make sure that your tax set-up is the most effective. The first issue is whether you are married: this will not affect your income tax (you are both treated separately), but it can make a difference to capital gains tax and inheritance tax, which are discussed in detail in the next chapter. If you are in a heterosexual relationship (as opposed to marriage or a same-sex civil partnership) your partner has no standing in the eyes of tax law – so you need to make a will and think about insurance if you get ill or have a car crash.

You also need to think about how your house is owned. If you are the owner, you need to make a will in order to protect your partner. If you own it jointly, you probably need to take advice on whether you should be joint tenants or tenants in common. The law will assume that you are joint tenants, but if you become tenants in common each of you in effect owns a separate 50%. This means that in your will you could leave your 50% to someone else – which can have advantages when you are making plans for inheritance tax.

The Right Income Tax Set-Up

So you work for a company, where your salary means that you pay some higher-rate tax. Your partner has given up her job to look after the children while they are young, but plans to go back to work later. At present, therefore, she pays no income tax.

Your first step is to make sure that all of your assets which produce an income are held by your partner. (Unless her dividend and interest income is so large that she also pays higher-rate tax.)

This means bank accounts, building society deposits, unit trusts and shares. If that makes you hesitate, then at least put all these into joint names, which the Revenue will assume means 50-50 unless you tell them otherwise. The logic is clear: interest which goes to your partner will not mean a tax bill – she will be able to claim back tax which the bank has deducted – while any interest you get will be taxed at 40%.

In this situation, it will make sense for you to take out a stakeholder pension for your partner. If you are self-employed and she helps you with your work, the premiums will be tax-deductible. If you are an employee, there is still a benefit as you will get basic tax relief on the contributions – £100 of premiums will cost you £80. (For detail, see Chapter 7 on pensions.)

Example: Save On Investment Income
Philip King and Tom Dodds have entered into
a civil partnership, which is taxed on the same
basis as if they were a married couple. Philip is a
successful lawyer, earning a salary of £50,000 a
year and he pays higher-rate tax; Tom is a teacher
and pays standard rate tax.

Philip has a savings income of £5,000 a year, on
which his tax bill amounts to £2,000. He decides
to put half of the investments into Tom's name
and they open a joint bank account into which
interest will be paid.

This means that half of the interest, or £2,500,
is now taxed as Tom's, on which he will pay tax
of 20% or £500. Philip pays £1,000 tax on his
remaining half, so the total tax bill has been cut
from £2,000 to £1,500. Putting the savings into
joint names has saved Philip and Tom £500 a
year.

Who Gives To Charity?

Your partner should not make donations by gift aid:
any charitable giving should be done by you. The
reason is simple: when you send money to a charity, it
is regarded as a net payment, so the charity will reclaim
the standard rate tax which is deemed to have been
deducted. As your partner has not paid any tax, the

Revenue will then demand from her the money it has handed over to the charity.

This is why most charities put a warning note on their gift aid forms, that you have paid sufficient tax to cover the amount which they will reclaim. If your partner insists that she make the donation to the charity, then she can ask the charity not to reclaim tax – this should work, though it's rather cumbersome.

Working For Yourself Is Different

If you are self-employed, the income tax rules offer you one great advantage over your salaried neighbour. This assumes, of course, that the Revenue accept that you are self-employed, and not an employee in disguise. There are a number of tests that the Revenue use – for example, do you control when and where you work – but probably the most effective is when you can show that you regularly work for different people.

Example: Expenses For Working At Home

Ed Abrey is an illustrator, who occasionally has to work from home; he is happy with the arrangement, as it means he can take some of the load off his wife who looks after their two young children. But Ed realises that there are costs when he works at home – he needs heat and light and he uses the phone for his work. As he is an employee, as opposed to being self-employed, he does not see how he can recover these expenses. ▶

Ed talks to his boss, who explains: he can readily pay Ed £100 a year free of tax, without the need for any back-up records. Ed explains that his expenses are bigger than that; his boss understands and is willing to pay more, which can also come free of tax – provided that Ed keeps records to support his claims. Ed starts keeping records!

The great advantage is that, as you are self-employed, you can pay a wage to your partner or spouse when they help with the business. These wages will be deducted from the profits of your business; as they pay little or no tax, while you pay 40%, this is a simple way for the family to save.

Paying your partner is appealing, but do not be over-ambitious. Whatever you pay must be reasonable for the work done and you will probably want to keep the payments below the point at which they will pay National Insurance and income tax and where you will have to pay employer's National Insurance. (You may think of employing your children – take care, as this can be illegal.)

Tax-Free Fringe Benefits

The self-employed have far greater flexibility than employees in being able to set expenses against their

Tax-Free Benefits For Employees

- Subsidised meals in a staff restaurant – if available to all employees.

- Loans of computers.

- Relocation costs if you are moving for your job.

- Staff sports and leisure facilities.

- Home phone line if there is a business need and minimum private use.

- Mobile phones, including line rental.

- Medical check-ups for you and your family – but not treatment.

- Workplace nurseries or play schemes.

- Pension information and advice.

- Gifts for long service.

- Suggestion scheme awards.

- Annual staff parties.

[NOTE: Some of these benefits are subject to a financial limit – e.g. staff parties must not cost more than £150 a head.]

income: their expenses have to be used 'wholly and exclusively' for their business, while an employee's have also to be used 'necessarily' – and the taxman decides what is necessary.

But there is still a variety of benefits open to an employee: if you use your own car for work, mileage allowance is tax-free so long as it does not exceed the Revenue's authorised scale; if you work for a financial organisation, a loan on favourable terms is tax-free up to £5,000 – and so on.

But How Do You Beat The Chancellor?

Assume that your family set-up has been arranged in a tax-sensible way – you still feel that you pay too much tax. How can you cut your tax bill?

The first answer has to be through making payments into a pension scheme, The financial year 2006–7 saw the start of generous new contribution rules which set the annual limit at the amount of your salary (indexed in line with inflation) so £235,000 for 2008–9. If you are an employee and the company scheme does not allow you to make large contributions, you simply set up your own plan (a SIPP, or self-invested pension plan) alongside.

But there are some risks in paying into a personal or group pension scheme.

How 500,000 Pension Savers Miss Out

Do you pay tax at higher rate? Do you pay into a personal or group pension scheme? If the answer to both questions is Yes, then there is a chance that you are missing out on tax relief – which you can claim back for six years.

Self-Assessment Needed

Informed estimates suggest that about half a million people are losing up to £1,000 a year each because they are not claiming their full tax allowance on pension payments. As you can carry back for six years (on the basis that you did not claim because you did not fully understand the regulations) this means that people have forfeited up to £6,000 each – which equals a massive £3 billion.

When you pay into a pension, you receive relief at the standard rate of tax – down from 22% to 20% – and this is added to your pension directly. If you pay tax at higher rate, at 40%, then you have to reclaim what is due to you. In a company pension scheme, you should be protected as your relief will be dealt with under PAYE – though there is nothing wrong in making sure by checking with your company's pension department.

The problem arises when you, the higher-rate taxpayer, are paying into a group scheme or a personal pension. To get the extra 20% relief to which you are entitled – doubling the amount you have already received – you have to file a self-assessment tax return.

Get A Tax Return

There are over 3 million people who pay higher-rate tax and about one-third of these – between 1 and 1.5 million – are reckoned to be paying into a personal pension. It is 500,000 of these, accountants believe, who are failing to claim the extra relief which is due to higher-rate taxpayers. These people may think they are getting their relief automatically, but they are not.

The suffering 500,000 probably believe that they are being given full higher-rate tax relief at source on their pension payments, so they think that they do not have to produce a tax return. Some taxpayers have even been told by the Inland Revenue that they do not need to file a self-assessment return because their tax affairs are 'relatively simple'.

Any higher-rate taxpayer who has been given this advice, and who makes pension contributions, needs to check that they are getting their full pension tax relief.

Example: Check On Your 40%

John Appleyard is a higher-rate taxpayer who pays the average amount into a personal pension plan – around £4,000 a year. He goes to an Independent Financial Adviser (IFA) who points out that he is entitled to 40% relief and that if he is getting only 20% then he is losing £800 a year, or £4,800 over six years.

The IFA points out that John's pension is also suffering: if John misses out on £800 a year over the 25 or 30 years of his working life, the impact on his pension will be serious. John rushes off to confirm that he is getting full 40% relief.

Join The Company Pension Scheme

If you are an employee, invariably the sound advice is to join the company pension scheme – if only because your employer will, almost always, also be contributing. On average, employers are estimated to pay in about 6% of salaries into the pension fund. If you ignore that and stay outside the scheme, you are effectively turning down a 6% pay increase.

There is a further refinement in joining the company pension scheme – sacrificing salary in order to improve your pension. You get tax relief on the contributions to the pension scheme and, as an important attraction, you save on National Insurance payments.

A variant on salary sacrifice is to arrange with your employer to have bonuses paid direct into your pension fund. This means that you will not have to pay tax on the bonus, while the employer will save on National Insurance – and he might be prepared to share that saving with you.

Think About a Venture Capital Trust

The Revenue give you tax breaks to invest in small companies. There are no guarantees that these investments will pay off – but on Venture Capital Trusts (VCTs) you get a 30% payback.

VCTs are finance companies which invest in small unquoted firms or shares that are listed on the Alternative Investment Market (AIM). You can buy up to of £200,000 worth of new VCT shares and get an income tax rebate of up to £60,000 even if you pay tax only at the basic rate – so long as you have paid the amount of tax which is covered in the rebate.

Hold For Five Years – But No Tax On Profits

You have to hold the shares for five years, but dividends come free of tax. Any profits you make from selling VCT shares will be exempt from Capital Gains Tax (CGT).

VCTs have to invest in small companies – their assets must not be more than £7 million and they must not employ more than 50 people. Small companies tend to suggest higher risk, but the supporters of VCTs say that many promising investments are in companies which have a low asset base, with the value embedded in intellectual property rather than physical plant and buildings.

Performance is not easy to measure, but if this type of investment appeals to you, then look at the managers' track record, their charges and dividend payouts.

Example: How To Give To Charity

Ed Lester wants to make a large donation to a cancer charity in memory of his late wife. He owns a small seaside flat, which cost him £50,000 and is now worth £150,000. His initial plan is to sell the flat and give the proceeds to the charity.

He does the sums: his gain is £100,000, so he will pay £18,000 in CGT. He could give the charity the remaining £132,000; as Ed is a higher-rate taxpayer, he would get a tax credit of £52,800. That all sounds fine, but his son Alec, who is a bright accountant, suggests a better way.

▶

His alternative is for Ed simply to donate his flat
to the charity. A donation to a charity is free from
CGT and he would get income tax relief on its
full market value – £60,000 as 40% of £150,000.
The charity would sell Ed's flat, giving them
£150,000. Everybody is happy with Alec's idea,
except perhaps the taxman.

Enterprise Investment Schemes

If you want to save yet more tax, and especially if you
want to cut back a capital gains tax liability, then think
about Enterprise Investment Schemes (EIS). EIS are
riskier than Venture Capital Trusts, but the potential
rewards are greater.

You can put £500,000 a year into EIS from 2008–9
and you get income tax relief of 20% or £100,000,
provided you hold the shares for at least three years
(five years in a VCT). Tax can be deferred on capital
gains realised in the three years before the EIS
investment or one year after. You could then rollover
the investment, and defer your capital gains bill yet
again and, as any banker will tell you, a liability
deferred is a liability reduced.

Capital gains tax is not due on any profits made from
the investment. Any losses – net of the initial income
tax relief – can be set against income or capital gains.

EIS shares are also exempt from inheritance tax once you have owned them for two years.

Trading Companies Only

EIS invest in a single small company worth less than £7 million and with fewer than 50 employees. EIS companies are not normally listed on a stock exchange and they must be trading companies, so that property, finance and hotels are excluded.

Many EIS have tended to be either film or pub businesses, but people are also looking at high-growth technology and biotechnology firms.

New Penalties For Tax Mistakes

If you put money into VCT and EIS schemes, the chances are that your tax affairs are big enough to justify going for professional advice. You may decide to go ahead by yourself, but just to emphasise the risks of making mistakes in dealing with the Revenue, a tough new penalty regime started to operate from the beginning of the 2008 tax year. Essentially, the Revenue has dropped the presumption that the taxpayer is innocent until proved otherwise; the burden of proof has been reversed.

Now, taxpayers are at risk if they pay too little tax or overstate a loss. You will have 30 days in which to establish an error in an assessment, or face penalties of up to 30% of the amount of the unpaid tax.

Example – When The Taxman Enquires

Jack Abrey is a worried man. His accountant tells him that the Revenue is making an enquiry into his tax return. This means that his return has been selected for further checking – either on the basis of a full enquiry or an aspect enquiry, when the taxman will focus on specific points. Jack will have to submit records to back the figures, including his bank statements.

It's six months since Jack sent in his return (and he was on time!); his accountant explains that since 2007–8 the Revenue must open an enquiry within a year of receiving your return. Jack cannot think of anything he has left out, but his accountant assures him that his return may have been selected at random. The taxman does not have to give a reason for the enquiry, though he may have received an anonymous tip-off about Jack's affairs or have some reason to believe that Jack has income he has not reported.

Jack is also worried how much all this is going to cost him in professional fees. His accountant tells him that the cost can be offset against tax – provided the Revenue do not find something which means that Jack has to face a further liability. If Jack is worried that this might happen again, he is told that it is possible to arrange insurance to cover the fees he will have to pay.

Guilty Until Proved Innocent?

The punch-line follows: there will be no penalty '. . . so long as the taxpayer has provided his accountant with accurate information and taken reasonable steps to check that the agent has made an accurate return . . .' The new threat lies in the last 14 words: you can no longer just rely on your accountant getting your return right from the information you gave him.

This represents a major shift, from the Revenue presuming taxpayers to be innocent to taxpayers having to demonstrate that they are acting properly. Accountants will become more careful and there are bound to be disputes between accountants and their taxpayer clients.

The Revenue say that they will not penalise taxpayers who have made mistakes that are not considered 'careless' or 'deliberate.' What we do not know is how the Revenue will define these two terms – and, above all, how they will determine when a taxpayer has been entirely innocent and is free from blame!

Example: When A Taxpayer Wants To Complain

Joe Smailes is angry. He thinks that his local tax office has been unreasonably slow in answering his questions. He raises his complaint with the woman who has been dealing with his case, but he is still unhappy.

▶

He next asks for contact details for the complaints manager. He gives details of all the delays, quoting his name and address, NI number and the Revenue's reference. Joe still feels he is getting nowhere, so he asks the director with overall responsibility for the tax office to review his complaint.

Joe thinks that the director himself is unreasonably slow in dealing with his complaint, so he goes to the independent adjudicator. The final step he could take is to ask his MP to refer his case to the Parliamentary Ombudsman.

Summary

- Two key rules – always tell the Revenue your details (date of birth, NI number, marital status) and always read what they send you.

- Think about your family set-up: suppose you are married, your wife looks after the kids so she has no income: she should be the one to hold shares and bank deposits, you should be the one to give to charity.

- Pensions are a great way to save – every pound into a pension cuts your tax bill at your top rate. A higher-rate taxpayer gets £100 worth of pension at a cost of £60.

♦ **Higher-rate taxpayers need to make sure they get all their relief on pension payments: they may need to make a separate return.**

♦ **You can cut your tax bill if you are prepared to make risky investments – in Venture Capital Trusts or Enterprise Investment Schemes.**

♦ **Be aware that the Revenue is getting tougher about mistakes, by you or your accountant. Assume you will be treated as guilty until you prove you are innocent.**

Chapter 5

And New Rules for CGT and IHT

The new rules for Capital Gains Tax (CGT) are simple: on the gains anybody makes, over and above the annual tax-free allowance – set at £9,600 for 2008–9 – the tax bill is 18p in the £. Forget about business and non-business gains, forget about taper relief and indexation allowance: you just pay 18%, which is slightly less than the standard tax rate of 20% and under half the higher-rate tax of 40%.

Under a U-turn earlier this year, a concession by the Chancellor brought in a 10% tax rate – as opposed to the normal 18% – for entrepreneurs on the first £1 million of gains they make during their lifetime. But the experts were not very impressed: for many entrepreneur taxpayers, the loss of indexation relief on long-held assets would still leave them worse off than under the old regime. And the Treasury narrowly defined an entrepreneur: you have to be a partner or director or hold more than 5% of the company's shares if you are an employee. Most people in SAYE schemes to not qualify.

Winners: Everyone who made a gain from selling a large holding of shares, or a second home; even if they paid standard rate tax, the size of their gain would probably push them into the higher-rate 40%, so that their tax bill is better than halved.

Losers: Every profit from selling a business asset now pays nearly twice as much tax. Under the old rules, a business gain was taxed at 25% of the profit if the asset had been held for more than two years – so that a higher-rate taxpayer would be charged only 10%. Now he has to pay 18%.

A whole range of business profits will be taxed more heavily, including gains you make from shares in the Alternative Investment Market (formerly business assets). The private equity executive who admitted that he paid less tax than his cleaner (he used to be liable for only 10%) will now pay more. Tax on buy-to-let will depend on whether you hold it personally or as a business: in the first case you win, in the second case you are worse off.

Income Into Capital

The first important lesson to draw from the new rules is that the CGT rate is slightly less than standard rate of income tax and much less than the higher rate. This means that if your profits come in the form of capital gains rather than income, you will be better off. A higher-rate taxpayer will keep £82 of a £100 capital gain, against £60 out of £100 of bank interest; a standard rate taxpayer will keep £82 against £80.

The simplest way to turn income into capital is to buy zero-coupon securities: these pay no interest but give a profit when they are repaid at a fixed date in the future – or if you sell them before then. In the UK, zero-coupon preference shares had a bad press in the early 2000s when a number of their sponsoring trusts went bust, but there is a range of attractive shares still on offer. If dollar investment appeals to you, there is a much larger number of zero-coupon bonds available in the USA and some also in the international market.

Buy a Bank Investment Plan

With a zero-coupon, neither your return nor your capital is guaranteed – as opposed to a bank investment plan, where you capital is secure. You cannot have security on both capital and profit: to be taxed as a capital gain, an investment must have an element of risk.

A bank plan works like this: over say five years, the plan will produce a deposit-type return of around 6% a year. This means that you will get £135 for every £100 you invested provided, for example, that the FTIndex is at least as high as when the plan started – and your £100 is meanwhile guaranteed by the issuing bank.

Your £35 gain will be taxed at 18% which amounts to £6.30. (Assuming that you have already used up

Table 5.1 How Tax Bills Compare: £1,000 gain on assets held for two complete years

	OLD TAX BILL	CURRENT TAX BILL
Business Gain:		
20% tax	£50	
40% tax	£100	
		£180
Private gain:		
20% tax	£200	
40% tax	£400	

[All gains in excess of annual allowance rates
effective 6 April 2008]

your annual CGT exemption). If you had placed the money on deposit you, as a higher-rate payer, would be charged 40% or £14, just over twice as much. The worst case under a bank investment plan is (perhaps unlikely) that at the end of the five years the FTIndex has fallen, so you just get your money back – you will have lost out to inflation.

You need to be aware that these plans run for pre-set periods, so there may be a penalty if you want to withdraw your money ahead of time. If you want to avoid tax altogether, it should be possible to put your plan into an ISA, so that all of the gain on a £7,200 investment would be free from tax.

Use Your Allowance

The second lesson from the new CGT rules is that you need to make active use of your annual tax-free allowance; the allowance does not run on – use it or lose it. Although the CGT rate of 18% is lower than income tax, you no longer have taper relief and the indexation relief: these former reliefs used to reduce the taxable gain or increase the base cost of your assets – which penalises people who have long-standing profitable investments.

There are essentially two ways to use your annual allowance: sell shares that you want to keep on which you have a gain and then buy them back, so that you crystallise the profit – or sell them and arrange for your wife or partner to buy a similar amount. Both routes work, but you need to handle the details with care: you should not buy shares back for at least 30 days after you sold and if your wife buys you need to make sure that the transaction is clearly arm's-length.

If you follow a sell and buy-back policy, it makes a great deal of sense to put your shares into joint names – you simply double your annual tax-free allowance. Nor do you need to be over-precise in your sell and buy-back programme: if you have a profit on a tracker unit trust, you can sell that and re-invest in another tracker – in that case you do not have to bother so carefully about the timing.

> **Example: CGT Losses And Married Couples**
>
> Fred Telfer is showing a loss on his BP shares, so he decides to sell them. But his wife, Janice, takes a positive view of oil shares; so, quite independently, she buys them back. (When this is planned, it is known as 'bed and spousing'). Fred puts the loss in his tax return, but his smart accountant sends out some warning signals.
>
> Fred's accountant explains that the Revenue have extended to individuals their rules which targeted companies trying to avoid tax by making use of capital losses, and might not allow Fred's loss. The accountant offers two pieces of advice: allow 30 days or more between Fred's sale and Janice's purchase, and he also suggests that Fred and Janice should not discuss these deals between themselves.
>
> Fred thinks this is absurd: is the message that husband and wife should not discuss their finances with each other? Well, says the accountant, the taxman is taking a wide view; he tells Fred and Janice to talk to him first if either of them thinks of another deal like this.

Who Pays CGT?

CGT becomes due when you sell or give away an asset – in the jargon, when you make a disposal. There is a range of exemptions to CGT, the most important being your own home – your 'principal residence'.

If you own more than one home, you have to nominate one as your principal residence – which you also have to do if you marry when you and your wife each owns a house. If you buy a second house, you can tell the Revenue within two years which is your main home, or they will make a practical assessment: any profits you make from selling a second home are subject to CGT (though there are ways of softening the blow – see later in this chapter)

Where Transfers Are Tax-free

There is no CGT to pay when assets are transferred between husband and wife nor between civil partners. A couple living together have to pay CGT on all transfers of assets – but they have a consolation: each of them can own a principal residence, where the gain will be tax-free when it is sold.

In principle, CGT covers gains which have been made since March 1982. Each year, every taxpayer gets a tax-free allowance – for 2008–9 the allowance was raised by £400 to £9,600. So, a couple who own shares in their joint names, can make gains of £19,200 in a year before they have to pay tax.

Tax-Free Gains

You may not expect to lose money on the sale of your

main home, but always remember: if the sale of an asset is free from CGT, then you get no allowance for losses. People who lose money on gilt-edged or on an ISA get no help from the tax system. If you do make losses, these can be carried forward.

Out of a long list of other exemptions from CGT, two of the most important are private cars and personal possessions which have a useful life of less than 50 years from the date you acquired them – such as a boat or a caravan.

Tax On a Take-Over

Apart from property – discussed later in this chapter – most people will have faced paying CGT when they sold shares or unit trusts.

But there is one trap you need to be aware of – when you hold shares in a company which is taken over. You can expect to get a premium over the stock market price, so that it becomes the sort of problem you may wish to have. But if the bid is in cash, you have made a disposal and face the prospect of paying CGT. This seems unfair to some people, as you did not choose to sell. There are four things you can do:

- Move the shares into joint names – if you have not already done so – to access £19,200 annual exemption: you just need to fill in the simple stock transfer form and post it to the company's registrars.

- If you are offered shares or cash in the company which makes the bid, take just enough cash to keep you below the CGT level. On the shares you will be given 'roll-over' relief; if you held 100 shares in Plastics plc and now have 150 shares in Superplastics plc, you have not made a disposal and the new 150 shares are given the same cost price as your original 100.

- You may be offered a loan note alternative. You are given a piece of paper which pays a modest rate of interest, normally around Bank of England base rate, and which you can cash in, say, over a five-year period. There is no disposal, because it is a paper-for-paper exchange which you can turn into cash when it suits your tax position – in effect, you have been given a form of bank deposit.

- If you are still facing a CGT bill, which you are not keen to pay, then you should realise available losses before the end of the financial year. If some of these losses are in shares you would like to keep, then sell them in the stock market and arrange for your partner to buy the same number. If you invested in an Enterprise Investment Scheme (see the previous chapter) then you can defer a capital gain up to the amount of your investment – and if you keep on investing, you can keep on deferring.

Saving CGT On Property

You may be one of the growing number who see

property as their pension. By 2008, share prices were
still below the level they reached at the end of 1999
– and many investors suffered badly in the dotcom
collapse which followed.

Just what do people mean when they say that property
is their pension? Look at some possible scenarios:

(a) You own a large house, which you sell, and you
     and your partner move into a flat. The profit from
     selling your house is tax-free as it is your principal
     residence and you use some of the proceeds to buy
     an annuity.

(b) You own a second home as well as the house you
     mainly live in. You go to live in your second home
     and sell your principal residence where the gain is
     free from CGT.

So far, so good: neither of these scenarios involves you
in CGT – but they do not fit every case. You may want
to sell your second home, in which case you will pay
CGT on the profit. You may be involved in buy-to-
let; unless you propose to live off the rental income,
you need to think carefully about CGT – if you sell
properties, plan to sell one a year to get the greatest
benefit from the annual exemption.

All the steps that save CGT on shares also apply to
property. If you put the property into joint names,
you get a double annual exemption; if you invest in an

Enterprise Investment Scheme, you can defer the tax; you can use losses to reduce the amount of gain.

But there are some special rules which apply to property, above all where you own a second home.

> **Example: Save CGT On Your Second Home**
>
> Simon Dawson is a financial IT manager who lives near his work at a flat in Canary Wharf. Years ago he elected this flat as his main home, i.e. principal residence. When he started to make a significant amount of money, he bought a house outside Brighton. He now wants to sell this house, but he stands to make a sizeable capital gain on which he will be taxed.
>
> Simon waits for the start of the new financial year, on 6 April, and changes his election so that the Brighton house is treated as his main home. Two weeks later, he changes the election back to the flat in Canary Wharf. Because the Brighton house has been his main home, even for a very short period, the gain which arises from the last three years of ownership are free from CGT.
>
> The cost is that when he comes to sell his flat the gain arising from the two weeks when it was not his main home will be subject to CGT.

Deeds of Variation

Anyone who stands to benefit from a will should remember deeds of variation. Under present rules (the experts have been expecting an official clampdown for some time) a will can be changed within two years of a person's death – provided there is agreement from everyone who benefits. Changes can also be made when someone dies without having made a will.

The other way a deed of variation is used is to re-route a legacy. When an adult receives a legacy they may decide it would be more tax-efficient for the legacy to go direct to their children. In this way, Inheritance Tax (IHT) at 40% will be saved on the amount of the legacy when they die.

IHT Will Cost Less

After the biggest change in 20 years, Inheritance Tax now offers a tax-free threshold (the nil rate band) of £624,000, rising to £700,000 in two years' time – at least for married couples and people in a civil partnership.

In theory, IHT is simple: the threshold is £312,000 for 2008–9, rising to £350,000 in 2010, and everything in the estate above that is taxed at 40%. The change, as from 9 October 2007, is that couples and civil partners will be able to transfer the unused element of the tax-free allowance to their spouse when they die. This means that when a husband dies and leaves all his assets to his wife, she will be able to leave up to £624,000 (£700,000 in two years' time), entirely free from IHT.

As with so many government moves, there is the good news and the not-so-good news:

Good news
- The new rules will be backdated indefinitely so that widows and widowers will be able to use their late partner's nil-rate band as well as their own when they die – about three million people are reckoned likely to benefit where the partner died perhaps many years ago and did not use any of their IHT allowance.

- The government has promised that in future the IHT nil-rate band will increase in line with house prices as well as inflation: this could be important – if the nil-rate band had followed house prices over the past 10 years the threshold would now be nearer £450,000.

Not-so-good news
- People who live together unmarried or outside a civil partnership will not benefit – nor will single people, those who are divorced or siblings who have lived together.

- Couples who have already made arrangements for their estates, by setting up trusts or using the nil-rate band, will be no better off (some trusts will be difficult to unwind) – the gainers from these changes are couples with sizeable assets who have not done any estate planning.

Example: Gainers From The New Rules

Jack Knott and his wife, Emily, own a house worth £350,000 and have other assets worth around £150,000. Before last October, Jack calculates that the IHT bill would have been £80,000 if they took no action – 40% of the amount by which their assets exceeded the threshold, i.e. £500,000 against £300,000 at that time.

Now, assuming that Jack dies first, Emily can access two thresholds (raised to £312,000 for 2008–9) and so will be able to pass on to their two children all of the £500,000 completely free from IHT.

Jack and Emily feel sorry for their neighbour Kate: she received the large house she lives in as part of her divorce settlement and now wonders how to pass it on to her daughter. Kate will get no help from the October 2007 changes; she reckons her house is worth about £600,000, so her estate will face a bill of over £100,000 when she dies.

How To Pass It On

Large numbers of people – especially single men and women and unmarried couples – will not gain from the October 2007 changes and still face the threshold, which gradually rises over the next few years. The typical house in London and the south-east is already worth as much as the threshold, and on average a detached house is worth rather more – about £326,000.

IHT can be a harsh tax: it has to be paid six months after the end of the month in which the death occurred, and is charged on world-wide assets, assuming that the person was domiciled in the UK. And all the former tax-free assets, such as ISAs and National Savings, are caught in the IHT net. So these people's thoughts turn to giving away assets in order to escape IHT. There are three principal ways:

- Small Gifts: In any tax year, you can give up to £250 each to any number of people and these gifts will be safe from IHT.

- Annual Exemption Gifts: You can give away £3,000 in IHT-free gifts every year – though you cannot combine these with a £250 gift to the same person. Husbands and wives each have a £3,000 limit and any unused part can be carried forward one year only, to the next tax year. (You can also make gifts, depending on the level of relationship, to anyone who is getting married.)

- Regular Gifts out of Income: This is potentially a very useful way to escape IHT. You can make regular cash gifts to someone so long as you can show that the gifts are habitual, are made from after-tax income and leave you with sufficient income to maintain your usual standard of living. If you want to give away any significant amount in this way, you should talk to an accountant.

- One message on making gifts: if you are giving away assets as opposed to cash, check first before you act to see whether you will have to pay any CGT.

Example: IHT Tax Break 'Backdated Indefinitely'

Joan Pickles' husband was killed in a car crash 10 years ago and he left her the flat where she now lives. She never remarried.

Joan is now pondering how to pass the flat, which is worth around £450,000, to her only son. She talked to an accountant some time ago, who told her that there would be an IHT bill of over £50,000 – which meant that her son would have to sell the flat. Following the October 2007 statement the accountant phoned Joan to explain that under the new rules she could now inherit her husband's IHT allowance, even though he died more than six years ago – which is the usual period set by the statute of limitations. This would give her £624,000 free from IHT in 2008–9, so her son could inherit the flat with no tax to pay.

Gifts – So Long As You Survive Seven Years

Outside the special tax-free categories, the gifts you make during your lifetime will escape IHT only if you survive for another seven years; these are known as Potentially Exempt Transfers.

If, alas, you do not survive the seven years then a taper system operates. The person receiving your gift (or your estate if they don't pay) will face the full 40% during the first three years, falling gradually to nil after seven years.

A Gift Is a Gift Is a Gift

Unless you make an outright gift, take care and take advice. The Revenue have been building a series of traps over recent years. These are the two most obvious:

- Gift with Reservation: This is where you give something away, but continue to benefit from it. A classic example is where you give your son the deeds of your flat, so that he becomes the owner, but you continue to live there. For IHT, the gift is simply irrelevant: to make the gift effective you either have to pay your son a market rent or go and live somewhere else.

- Pre-owned Assets: If you still use something which you have given away since March 1986 and you do not fall foul of the gift with reservation rules, you may be caught by this test. Suppose, back in 1987, you gave your son some shares which have rocketed in value. He sells the shares and uses some of the money to buy you a flat – then you will be caught.

Time For Trusts?

Only a few years ago, any advice on avoiding IHT would have included a long section on trusts. Following the Chancellor's clampdown in his 2006 Budget anyone planning to put a large amount into trust needs to take professional advice.

Example – Pre-Owned Asset Tax: It Can Pay Not To Be Married

Ed and Judy are an unmarried couple who live in Ed's large house in Surrey. Ed had to retire because of ill-health and is thinking about raising money on the house through a partial equity release. Judy is a successful City lawyer, and she suggests to Ed that she should buy part of the house, which they will continue to live in.

Ed is delighted, but he is concerned over Pre-Owned Asset Tax (POAT), which arises if you continue to use something which you have given away or sold for less than full market value at any time since March 1986.

▶

Judy talks to one of her partners who explains:
if Judy were, say, Ed's daughter or sister, the
proposal would be caught for POAT. Ed would
have to sell the house at its open market value
and pay market rent while he is living there.
But as Ed and Judy are not married, they are not
'connected' in the eyes of the tax laws – so there is
no POAT to pay!

Smaller trusts have escaped the new rules – where
over seven years you plan to invest no more than
£312,000 (the IHT limit for 2008–9) into trust. Some
trust schemes are becoming available again – such as
discounted gift trust and loan trust schemes. These can
be especially helpful where there is an IHT liability but
people are unable to make outright gifts because of the
need to maintain income.

Example: A Trust to Save IHT

Alan King is aged 70, with an estate valued at £1
million. That will mean an IHT bill of £275,000
(at 2008–9 rates). Alan is advised to invest
£250,000 into a discounted gift trust and to
reserve the right to an income of £1,000 a month
(this is regarded as a return of capital for tax
purposes and so gets to Alan tax-free).

Alan has to survive for seven years to get the full benefit of the scheme, but even if he dies within that time there will be a useful saving. If he survives for seven years, then the whole gift trust fund of £250,000 would go to his beneficiaries free of IHT. That represents a saving of £100,000 (40% of £250,000), which makes Alan very content.

Bare Trusts Escape

Parents wanting to invest for their children's future will be relieved that the Government has decided not to tax bare trusts. These are set up, often by finance companies, to ensure that the child cannot access the money until age 18. Gifts into bare trusts rank as 'potentially exempt transfers' so the giver has to survive for another seven years to avoid IHT.

Bare trusts are popular as a low-cost and effective way of handing down money. But parents must remember that they will pay tax if the income goes above £100 a year. So invest in tax-free assets or arrange for the money to come from someone else – in that case the rules do not apply.

While Older Trusts Suffer

Accumulation and Maintenance trusts used to be a popular with parents and grandparents who wanted, say, to keep control of the trust's income until the child reached 25 – and capital for up to 80 years. Now, A&M trusts escape tax only if the assets go to the child at age 18. Trustees can keep control until age 25, but there is a 4.2% tax after the child's 18th birthday.

Interest in Possession trusts were used to pass capital down to children but provide an income for the widow or widower. In the 2008 Budget, you now have until October 2008 (a six month extension) to change these trusts to comply with new law.

Summary

♦ **Everyone now pays the same rate of CGT – 18%. The difference between business and private assets has been scrapped, along with taper relief and indexation allowance. Capital gains are now more valuable than income.**

♦ **Married couples and civil partners can double to £624,000 the IHT-free element in their estates – rising to £700,000 in two years' time. But heterosexual couples, divorc(e)es and family members get no benefit.**

- Your own home is free from CGT, so you pay no tax on the profit from its sale. If you own two houses, you should tell the Revenue which is your 'principal residence'.

- You get a tax-free allowance for CGT each year – £9,600 for 2008–9. The allowance doubles when you own assets jointly with your partner, but it does not carry over from one year to the next: use it or lose it.

- If you own a second home, you will be liable for CGT if you sell. But you can reduce the bill by turning it into your main home, even for a very short time.

- To reduce your estate for IHT, think about making gifts: you can use the £3,000 a year allowance – or talk to your advisers about making regular gifts out of income which do not affect your standard of living.

- Setting up small trusts can still work – up to the nil-rate band over seven years – but get advice if you want to do more.

- If you inherit, remember that you can change a will within two years by a deed of variation – provided that all the beneficiaries agree.

Chapter 6

The Fifth Way – Invest With Care

You have put your household affairs into good shape, you have created a cash buffer for emergencies, so you start to think about investing. First, you have to decide what you are aiming to achieve: a bundle of assets which in five, 10 or maybe even 15 years' time will enable you to achieve your key ambition – pay school fees, travel round the world, buy a house in France, whatever.

So where do you place your surplus income? The starting-point for many people will be National Savings: they are backed by the government, so virtually risk-free and readily available over the internet or by walking into your nearest post office.

National Savings really break into two classes, Premium Bonds and then a series of other investments some of which are attractive, but many of which are not. Premium Bonds are a lottery where your money capital is safe; you are gambling only with the interest.

A Gamble On Premium Bonds

When money goes into Premium Bonds – each of us is allowed to hold £30,000 worth – a rate of interest is paid to generate the monthly prize money. When this was written, the rate was 3.8%, which was paid out in the form of two prizes of £1 million each, plus a range of smaller prizes. The smallest prize is £50 and if you win the chances are 9 out of 10 that you will get either £50 or £100; minimum holding is £100.

The odds are that, if you hold the maximum £30,000, you will get a prize a month. This depends on the notion of 'average luck'; if your luck comes out differently, you may go months without a prize or win the bonanza £1 million straight away. All the prizes come tax-free and do not even have to be reported to the Revenue. Like any tax-free investment, Premium Bonds are worth more to higher-rate taxpayers.

Some people regard Premium Bonds as the first essential part of an investment portfolio. Others ignore what is after all a lottery and some will buy a few hundred pounds' worth just for the (slim) chance of a big win. This has to be a matter for your own taste.

If you buy any sizeable amount of Premium Bonds, it makes sense to track them like any other investment: work out what you receive over, say, 12 months and if you are not getting 3.8% then you should probably count yourself unlucky and you may well decide to cash in. National Savings will send you a cheque when you win and you can always check your prizes on their website.

Choice of Certificates

Outside Premium Bonds, probably the most popular National Savings products are Savings Certificates – but you need to take on board the tax situation. Certificates come in two forms, fixed-rate and index-linked, and both are tax-free. If you pay no tax, you can do better elsewhere; if you pay tax at the standard 20% rate the decision is marginal; if you pay tax at the higher 40% rate the certificates, especially index-linked, are potentially attractive.

Index-linked certificates pay a premium on top of inflation, over three or five years. When this was written, the three-year certificates offered inflation plus 1.15% compounded, and the five-year inflation plus 1.1%. An individual can hold £15,000 worth of each issue, and a husband and wife can double up.

Example: National Savings Or Not?
Jack Aspinall and his wife Greta worry that inflation will cut back the real value of their pensions, so they think about putting their savings into three-year index-linked National Savings certificates. Jack has a final salary pension and pays tax at 40%; Greta, who is on a teacher's pension, pays standard rate of 20%.

Jack does a sum: he reckons that 4.15% tax-free is worth just under 6.9%. This is better than he can get in the market, and the risks are low; in his view, this makes up for the lack of liquidity – no interest from the certificate if he has to cash in during the first year.

For Greta, a tax-free 4.15% equates to just under 5.2% before tax. She checks the internet and realises that she can do better than that with an instant access account offered by one of the major financial groups.

Jack buys the index-linked certificates, but Greta puts her money with a bank.

What To Hold In an ISA

The Individual Savings Account (ISA) is the other tax-free concession which the Government offers you. This is not a product, like a bond or a certificate from National Savings; it is a wrapper, into which you can put shares and unit trusts and pay no further tax. But you need to be careful about the investments you place in an ISA wrapper.

The ISA rules have improved since April 2008. ISAs have been given an indefinite life and you can now put

£7,200 in each financial year into your ISA – £3,600 of this can be in cash. All the old titles have been changed, so there are now just 'cash ISA accounts' and 'stocks and shares ISA accounts'. If you hold PEPs from pre-1999, these will become 'stocks and shares ISAs' and TOISAs (from old TESSA schemes) will be 'cash ISA accounts'. Child trust funds can be rolled over into ISAs when they mature.

You can open a cash ISA at 16 – a useful present for the kids – and a shares ISA at 18; you have to be a UK resident, and ISAs do not have to appear on your tax return. One new concession: you can move your existing cash ISA into a stocks and shares ISA and this will not count against the year's allowance. (You can't do the opposite and turn a shares ISA into cash.) If you move abroad, you can keep the ISAs you already hold but you cannot make any new investments.

Choose The Type Of Fund

To start with, put any money on deposit (or in your emergency fund) into a cash ISA. This is a no-brainer: you will get the interest free of tax, against being subject to tax – so surprising that Ministers say 67% of UK households are missing out on ISA tax breaks

You then need to look at capital and income separately. There is no CGT to pay when you sell shares or unit trusts at a profit – but how often are you likely to exceed your annual tax-free allowance? So the freedom from CGT will probably matter to people who have larger investment portfolios.

Income is more complex: essentially, if you are a basic rate taxpayer you should hold bonds in your ISA and ordinary shares outside. This goes back to the time Gordon Brown stopped ISA managers from reclaiming the 10% tax which is deducted from dividend payments on ordinary shares. By contrast, an ISA manager can still reclaim the 20% tax which is paid by bond funds (minimum 60% in bonds).

On ordinary share dividends, this is how it works:

- Basic rate taxpayers: no saving by holding shares in an ISA;

- Higher-rate taxpayers: a moderate saving – if they held the shares outside an ISA, they would have to pay further tax on the dividends.

So – put bonds into your ISA where possible and hold equities outside.

Example: Appeal Of Multi-Manager Funds

Richard Grainger has built up a portfolio of unit trusts, both in ISAs and outside. He favours multi-manager funds, where a professional fund manager chooses a range of funds which gives a particularly wide selection of underlying holdings. Richard specifies his area of interest and leaves the manager to do the rest – which he reckons is worth the slight extra cost through paying two sets of annual management charges.

One of Richard's direct unit trust holdings turned out to be the top-performing fund over the last five years – showing a rise of a staggering 388%. Richard knows that average fund performance over the same period was just 41%, which convinces him it is vital to obtain independent research from a trustworthy source.

How About a DIY ISA?

ISAs substantially hold unit trusts – how you buy these is discussed later in the chapter. But for some people, buying a unit trust is like buying a package; they prefer to choose their own investments.

You can opt for a self-select ISA: you will have to pay the manager, who will generally be a bank, an administration fee, say £30 a year for one ISA and

£60 a year for larger amounts. You will probably get a concessionary rate on buying shares – this is important, because you cannot just transfer shares which you own into an ISA. You will need to sell them and buy them back within the ISA. The manager will probably collect dividends for you and allow you to make periodic payments if you want to buy new shares.

A Place For Unit Trusts

A large part of the UK's adult population hold ISAs, and a large part of their ISA investments are held in unit trusts. The theory of unit trusts is simple – and the same applies to their modern successors, OEICs or open-ended investment companies. An organisation sets up a portfolio of investments and creates, say 1 million units, and divides these among unit-holders who are all equal; if unit-holders want to sell, the number of units falls and if people want to buy, the number increases.

A unit trust manager will point out the advantages:

- Spread your risk. A typical unit trust portfolio will contain several dozen, possibly a hundred or more, different shares so you avoid the great investment mistake – putting all your eggs in one basket. Against this, a wide spread of shares is unlikely to produce sensational performance.

- Expert management. Specialist full-time fund managers watch over the portfolio. This raises the immediate question: how good are these full-time managers? Fund management groups vary a good deal in performance, so you need to monitor, say every six months, how your groups are doing.

- Specialisation. If you believe in the future of, say, small companies or the economy of Brazil, then a unit trust represents an attractive vehicle. You need a spread of risk and expert judgement – but you have to monitor performance particularly closely when you depend so much on the manager's skills.

Property: Go Buy A REIT

Most people appreciate the case for including real estate as part of their total portfolio: according to the Halifax index, the average UK house price has risen by 2.8 times over 10 years. That represents a healthy annualised appreciation of 10.7%, well ahead of inflation. Over the same period, the FTSE all-share index showed an average annual growth of just 4.6% – less than half as good.

Until now, the problem has been how to invest in property? Your own house represents a substantial property investment, but not everyone wants to buy a second home while buy-to-let requires some specific skills. Buying shares in property companies just brings you back into the all-share index.

But since 2007, investors have had an alternative: the REIT, or Real Estate Investment Trust. In a REIT (originally invented in the USA during the 19th century), the company agrees to pay out at least 90% of its profits through shareholder dividends, and in return becomes largely free from corporation tax. The great benefit for shareholders is the ending of double taxation (corporation tax on the company plus the tax on dividends) so that your investment is much closer to going into property direct.

Major UK property companies promptly turned themselves into REITs, including Land Securities and British Land, and there now around 20, all listed and offering a spread of property interests and liquidity: you just buy and sell the shares, which can be easier than trading in property unit trusts and OEICs. You can put REIT shares into an ISA or a Self-invested Personal Pension (SIPP).

Shareholders are likely to receive two payouts – 90% of the profits from the REIT's tax-exempt property rental business, plus a traditional-type dividend from other activities. Overall, the creation of REITs has upped the level of payouts to shareholders.

Choice of Sectors

The larger unit trust groups have tended to follow the principal investment sectors: you can buy growth trusts, which offer small yields but the prospect of capital appreciation; equity income trusts, which offer above-average yields; special situation trusts, where the managers look for undervalued shares and bond funds, especially popular among ISAs, where the assets consist of fixed-interest stocks issued by governments and companies.

Unit trust and OEIC managers provide 'active' performance: their experts try to outperform the average of their particular sector. When you assess performance, that is the benchmark you should use, along with the performance of the stock market as a whole. If the trust performs well against its sector, but poorly against the market, then you have probably made the wrong choice of sector.

Rise of the Tracker

Comparison of your unit trust against the stock market is a basic test, not least because nowadays you have an easy way to replicate stock market performance – through the tracker fund. These are unit trusts which reproduce the performance of the London and New York stock markets, as well as Europe and Japan, and even sectors within those markets: in London you can buy tracker units for the top 100, 250 and 350 companies.

The first appeal of trackers is that they are low-cost, as they run on a fixed portfolio or a computer program. You can buy trackers of the London stock market which charge no initial fee and where the annual cost is 0.5% or below. This is a good deal less than the typical actively managed fund – even if you save on buying costs, as explained below.

How Well Do Managers Manage?

A good active manager will out-perform a tracker – and there are some large funds whose performance is ahead of their benchmarks. But people have begun to worry that this is not typical, and that the average fund manager may not, over a period, even keep up with the market.

Table 6.1 shows a piece of research produced by a London financial group.

Active managers do well in specific sectors, such as UK small companies, or geographic areas, such as Japan and the Far East where a UK private investor simply does not have enough information to make sensible investment decisions. It is in the key general areas, such as UK All Companies, that trackers outperform active managers. Part of the reason may be the costs of share dealing (notably stamp duty), but the moral seems to be:

Table 6.1: Average percentage of actively managed funds beating the Index over rolling three-year periods

Spanning 20 years

Sector	Index	Average
UK All Companies	FTSE All-Share	35%
UK Equity Income	FTSE All-Share	47%
UK Small Companies	FTSE Small Cap	66%
Global Growth	MSCI World	44%
Europe ex UK	FTSE Europe ex UK	45%
North America	S&P 500	31%
Asia Pacific ex Japan	MSCI Ac Far East ex Japan	59%
Japan	FTSE Japan	52%

Source: Bestinvest.

- Choose a good active manager in a specialist area, monitor his performance -including staff changes, and

- For general investment, put money into tracker funds – and make sure that you choose the lowest cost: trackers may be cheaper than active funds, but some trackers are cheaper than others.

Ask About Save-As-You-Earn

If you work for a company which is listed on the stock exchange, it's worth asking about Save-as-you-Earn

(SAYE). You save a fixed amount, between £5 and £250 a month, and at the end of three or five years the cash is used to buy shares at a 20% discount – based on the share price when the scheme started.

The great appeal of SAYE is that you cannot lose. You have an option to buy the shares when the contract is complete, but you can just take your money and walk away. This means that you will make a handsome profit if the shares go up and you get your money back if they drop: for any investor, that is a no-brainer.

Even if you leave the company, you get your money back and you may still be able to buy the shares. Scheme rules vary, but in general you should get six months to buy the shares (assuming they show a profit), so long as you are at least three years into the contract. SAYE is one of the casualties of the October 2007 budget – gains are now taxed at 18%, against 10%, for higher-rate taxpayers. But an investment where you cannot lose, and you might gain, still has its attractions.

How To Buy Unit Trusts

Like any good consumer, you first check relative prices, where you will find that the most expensive trusts are managed, especially if they focus overseas, while trackers are the cheapest. You make your choice, and your initial decision is to contact the fund manager. But this is the most expensive way to buy unit trusts!

A typical managed unit trust will charge around 5% on your initial investment and make an annual charge of 1.5%. If you buy £10,000 worth of units, this means you will pay out £650 in charges during the first 12 months – which will probably wipe out most of the first year's growth.

Instead, you can go to a fund supermarket or a discount broker; brokers use supermarkets and some operate their own. The key here is that the manager's initial 5% includes a sales commission, and the supermarket/broker will share that with you to get your business. You should be able to reduce the 5% to 1%, or even less.

Some brokers will offer you a ready-made package of unit trusts – such as income, cautious growth and aggressive growth – at prices which give a discount on the initial and annual charge. If you are uncertain about investment choice, these packages will appeal as they give you both a spread of units and benefits from discounting.

The manager's annual charge also includes a payment to the salesman so long as you hold the units. Some brokers will divide this 'trail' commission with you, and some will give you a fixed rebate, of say, 0.25%. Sharing of trail commission has developed over the past few years, and you may need to look carefully to find a broker who will oblige: but if you are a long-term holder, this saving could be well worthwhile.

You can't expect significant savings on the low-cost
funds, such as a tracker. But some specialised trackers
cost more and you may be able to find a concession.
Always ask!

Why Gentlemen Prefer Bonds

Time was when serious and cautious investors bought
with profit bonds from insurance companies. These
bonds, which were invested in a conventional mix of
ordinary shares, property and bonds, paid growing
bonuses and smoothed out fluctuations in the stock
market. Many people still hold these bonds.

All this came to a grinding halt in the market collapse
of 2000–3: the companies paid out bonuses during
three years of falling markets, which was just when
the FSA compelled the insurance companies to sell
shares and switch into bonds. You may have suffered
from the MVR, the market value reducer, which many
companies introduced to deter people who wanted
to exit. If this is your problem, look carefully for
MVR-free dates – these are typically on 5th and 10th
anniversaries, and sometimes each subsequent 5th
anniversary. If you think you might want to leave, these
are important dates not to miss. (If in doubt, check the
policy document).

But you may be a strong-minded contrarian: doing
the opposite of most other people has often proved a
successful investment strategy. So, if you are minded to

move into with-profit bonds, you should do two things.
First, you should buy through a discount broker, not
direct. Secondly, you should look for the insurance
companies which have the largest equity percentages
– these offer the best growth prospects for the years
to come. You need to do your homework, because
some major companies cut their equity holdings to
less than half their total portfolio. But on a recent
analysis, Liverpool Victoria showed the highest equity
proportion with the Prudential, which has low average
MVR rates, one of the majors to hold above 50%.

Bonds For Income

If you do not want to take any risks with your capital,
and were considering an investment in a building
society, think about guaranteed income bonds.
Insurance companies offer these bonds with a fixed
income and a return of capital and they normally run
for between one and five years, with three-year bonds
generally the most popular. The key to buying these
bonds is that you invest when interest rates are high, so
that you can lock in an appealing return.

The minimum investment may be set higher than a
building society, say £5,000, but there is the flexibility
that higher rates will be paid on larger amounts. You
should be able to choose whether you want income
paid yearly or monthly. One feature is that, because
these bonds are an insurance product, there is no limit
to compensation if the company hits difficulties – at

a building society compensation is capped at just over
£30,000.

Because the bonds are an insurance product, interest
is paid net of basic rate tax – a point which is often
overlooked when people look through comparison
tables. If a bond offers, say 4.5%, a basic rate taxpayer
pays no more tax and is getting a gross return equal to
5.6%.

Bonds Which Distribute

If you are prepared to face a rather bigger risk, in
return for possible capital growth, think about
distribution bonds. These are issued by major insurance
companies, with a typical minimum of £5,000 or
£10,000. The bonds are invested in a mix of shares,
bonds and commercial property – but your income and
capital are not guaranteed.

Distribution bonds can carry higher charges than
income bonds, so you need to look for a discount
broker. Yields will often be slightly higher than income
bonds and income is paid net of basic rate tax.

But there is an important tax gimmick for higher-rate
payers – the same sort that attracted so many people
to with-profit bonds over the years. This is that if you
keep income to 5% or less, you will not have any more
tax to pay for up to 20 years or until you cash in the
bond. Your withdrawals are free of income tax and do

not even count as income, so there are no problems which might affect your state benefit or age allowance. (People over 75, for example, begin to lose their age allowance, set at £9,180 for 2008–9, once their income exceeds £21,800.)

One word of caution: when you take your 5% a year, you need to be sure that you are not eating into your capital: in other words, that the underlying fund is performing better. This means that you need to keep a watch, say every three or six months, to see how the managers are performing.

Bonds Which Lie Offshore . . .

Offshore bonds are generally attractive to higher-rate taxpayers. They work like the onshore variety: you make a lump-sum investment, often with a minimum of £10,000 and you can withdraw up to 5% a year free of tax. If you work abroad, or plan to retire overseas, you may be able to cash in free of tax.

The big difference from an onshore bond is that the onshore fund manager has to pay tax on gains which are made within the fund. In an offshore bond, the gains can roll up in a substantially tax-free environment.

For basic-rate taxpayers there is no great advantage in going offshore: an onshore bond pays out net of basic rate tax. An offshore bond may produce bigger gains, but these will be subject to income tax. Higher-rate taxpayers will generally be more interested in the freedom to switch funds without paying CGT and in the ability to gift offshore bonds without creating a tax liability.

. . . And Turn Into a Roll-Up Fund

You can put cash into an offshore bond wrapper, rather than going into an investment fund, which gives you a roll-up fund of the type managed by a number of banks. In these funds, interest rolls up as opposed to being paid out and you do not have any tax to pay until you cash in.

Buying a Protected Bond

1. You invest a minimum £5,000.
2. You hold the investment for 5.5 years.

Protection: Your money capital is safe.
Growth: You get up to 110% of the growth in the 100 share index – capped at 50% of your original investment.

But: You receive no dividends.
If you have to cash in early, you may not get back all your original stake.

So, if you are a higher-rate taxpayer who becomes a basic-rate payer when you retire and cash in, you will be liable for 20% tax on the accumulated interest rather than 40% – which you would have paid if you had put your money into an onshore bank or building society. And the roll-up fund is useful if you have specific commitments in the future, and if you are the kind of person who likes to decide just how much tax he pays and when.

Small and Friendly

If tax-free investment appeals to you, there is another, small possibility: saving with a friendly society. Anyone over age 16 can save up to £25 a month; this is invested in a with-profits fund consisting typically of shares, fixed interest bonds, property and cash. Your money grows free of income tax and CGT, and there is no tax to pay on your profits when you cash in.

A family of four could save £100 a month but you need to realise that this is not a short-term or liquid investment. Your money goes into a 10-year bond; when you start you are quoted a guaranteed cash sum. Growth comes through added bonuses – which once given, cannot be taken away. But if you have to cash in during the early years, you may get back less than you contributed.

Friendly societies have two things going for them: investment in them is virtually as safe as in National Savings, and friendly societies' performance should be rather better than a building society. One of the larger societies managed 5% annual growth over a recent 10-year period – so someone saving £25 a month would at the end of the term have been given a cheque for just under £3,900.

Not earth-shattering, but not bad from an investment which you can start and then forget about until it matures.

Summary

♦   **Premium Bonds: you gamble with your interest – your money capital is safe. With average luck, you will get 3–4% on your money: all prizes are tax-free and do not even have to be reported to the taxman.**

♦   **Savings certificates, especially index-linked, appeal to higher-rate taxpayers. Standard ratepayers can do rather better in the market and non-taxpayers much better.**

♦   **ISAs are a tax-free wrapper in which you can place a range of assets – most usefully bond unit trusts, where the managers can reclaim tax that has been deducted. Except probably for higher rate-taxpayers, shares should be held outside an ISA.**

- Unit trusts allow you to spread your risk and to access expert management– useful if you decide to invest in the 'new' economies such as China and Brazil. You need to monitor performance against the index and against the peer group; you also need to watch for changes in senior personnel.

- Tracker unit trusts follow particular stock markets, at much lower costs than managed unit trusts. Research suggests that, outside specialised sectors, trackers do better than managed funds.

- Keep down the cost of buying unit trusts by going to a discount broker or a fund supermarket. If you go direct to the manager, you could pay much of the first year's growth.

- If tax-free investments appeal to you, think about Friendly Societies: though the limit is £25 a month, anyone over 16 can join. This should be regarded as a 10-year investment.

Chapter 7

The Sixth Way – Think Outside The Box

Every week, sometimes every day, a take-over bid is launched for a public company, bringing a dramatic rise in the share price – increases of 50% or more, even in the shares of large companies, often happen. How do you, the average investor, get a piece of the take-over action?

The first answer is to buy shares in companies which will be taken over. Alas, there is no simple recipe: some people buy shares in a large company when its profits fall – but there is the underlying assumption that a take-over will solve its problems.

For the average investor, three ideas can be useful:

1. Buy shares in a company where a take-over bid was made, but failed. The frustrated bidder may negotiate with the board – especially if the failed bid was hostile – and then bid again. And the failed bid may rouse interest from other

companies in the same sector: they may see assets of the bid victim that were not previously obvious, or they may just want to keep out the bidder who failed. In that case, one of them may launch a bid.

2. Buy shares in a company where another company owns a large but not controlling interest.
   That may be a blocking interest, designed to keep competitors away, but in many cases the shareholding company may decide that it wants complete, not just partial, control. This rule works best when the shareholder is another industrial company, where the benefits from integration will be greater than for a financial investor.

3. Buy shares in a company when a bid is announced. This is a technique used by some professional investors, based on the view that the stock market can over-state the uncertainties (will the board agree? will the government order an inquiry?), which can prove particularly profitable if a bidding contest develops. There is the risk that the bid fails, so the share price falls – though it will probably stay higher than before the bid was made.

How To Buy and Sell Shares

To buy and sell shares you need a stockbroker who trades in shares on the London Stock Exchange and – perhaps – AIM.

Before you go to a broker, you need to form some broad view of how you are likely to trade:

- Will you buy small and medium-sized amounts of shares steadily, aiming to build a portfolio, or;

- Will you generally buy a series of shares and then aim to sell in a few months' time in one transaction, or;

- Will you trade often, perhaps even become a 'day trader' where you buy and sell shares within one trading day?

Brokers' charges vary a good deal, and you need to tailor the way you operate to what you are paying for.

Execution-only brokers have become popular: they do not give advice, but simply process the transactions you specify (some will provide investment data). Most of these brokers operate on a nominee basis, where they hold your shares electronically rather than send you a paper certificate. [Note: this may cause a problem if you want to access shareholder perks – you will need both the broker and the company to agree.]

▶

You will find:

- Online dealing is cheaper than telephone dealing.

- Deals through nominee accounts are cheaper than using paper share certificates; you will probably not have to pay to move shares into a nominee account, but there will be a charge if you want to withdraw.

- Dividends are easy to handle: the broker will keep them in a cash account, or send them to your bank or use them to buy into an agreed share.

Costs:
+ Commission, which is charged as a percentage of the deal amount or as a flat fee irrespective of the deal size;

+ Annual fee: the broker may charge you for holding your shares and some will charge you if you go inactive for a period, and

+ Official charges which are 0.5% stamp duty on the amount involved in a purchase; for larger ordinary share deals over £10,000 there is a £1 levy to finance the City Takeover Panel.

[Note: if you are buying or selling shares in a leading company, first check to see if they have set up a low-cost dealing facility with a named broker; this will cut your costs.]

Frequent dealers should consider:

- Limit Orders: where you set upper and lower prices at which you are prepared to deal, and;

- Stop-Loss Orders: where you fix a price at which, when the market falls, you give an automatic sale instruction. These can save you a lot of money if the stock market suddenly falls.

Key terms

CREST: the UK automated settlement system, which allows shareholders and bondholders to hold assets electronically – rather than physical paper share certificates.

Nominee Account: where a named holder, often an execution-only broker, holds assets on behalf of someone else, known as the beneficiary. This speeds up settlement: no one has to wait for paper to be moved around. Your shares are registered in the broker's name, making him the legal owner, but you are the beneficial owner.

Stocks and Shares: 'stock' used to mean that the shares or bonds had to be transferred in units of £100, e.g. Preference stock rather than Preference shares – nowadays 'shares' covers all.

[Also see Glossary]

Funds For 'Special Situations'

If you feel you do not have the time or the resources to follow companies in a proactive way, there is the option of buying into a unit trust, which does the same thing. These are the 'special situations' funds, where managers look for companies that are vulnerable to a take-over or which have been undervalued by the stock market.

The outstanding fund in this group was Fidelity UK Special Situations, run by Anthony Bolton for nearly 20 years, which grew to £3 billion and out-performed both its peer group and the stock market index. Now, all the major fund groups offer special situations, dynamic or recovery unit trusts, which can be bought in the usual way, through an adviser/broker or online.

In these trusts, management is key. You need to watch especially carefully how the funds perform and in particular when management changes.

Bet On a Bid

If you like to place bets, you can bet on a take-over. This is spread-betting, which enables you to bet on how a share price will move: you need to put only a small amount of cash up-front, while any profits you make will be free of CGT. Most spread-betting is done online.

Example: How Spread-Betting Works

Dennis Brookes likes to bet. He believes that
Anvil United will receive a take-over bid, so that
the share price will rise.

He goes to a spread-betting firm which quotes
the shares at 100/102p. This means he can buy
at 102p and he decides to gamble £10 on every
point, or lp, movement upwards.

Dennis' scheme works. The bid for Anvil United
arrives, and the shares are now quoted at 120/
122p.

Dennis cashes in: he sells at 120p, which gives
him an 18-point gain. His bet was £10 a point, so
he makes a profit of £180 – and all free of tax.

But, if the share price falls, you will lose money: there
is no safety net unless you create one. This is why many
investors take out a stop-loss provision, so that their
shares are sold automatically if the price falls to a pre-
determined level; you lose, but your loss is limited.

Gain Through a Hedge Fund

Hedge funds have become major players in world
financial markets, and their attractions (and the
opposite) are discussed in the next section. In take-
overs, hedge funds have developed specific skills, so

if you want to share in this action then you should consider buying into hedge funds.

Here is one example of how a hedge fund can operate: when Company A bids for Company B, shares in Company A may fall. The stock market may think the price is too high, or that the strategy is misguided; Company A may be offering shares, so that dealers fear a short-term glut.

In this case, the hedge fund will 'go short': it will borrow shares in Company A from insurance companies and pension funds and then sell them. Assuming its judgment is correct, and Company A shares fall, the hedge fund will buy back the shares at the lower price, pay off its loan and pocket a useful profit.

Should You Buy Hedge Funds?

This take-over example may give you a taste for hedge funds – in which case you are far from lonely. Hedge funds are now big business, with around 9,000 funds world-wide managing £750 billion or so of investors' money, usually from pension funds and wealthy individuals who are experienced stock market investors.

Hedge fund managers often prefer to be known for 'absolute return funds', which seek to achieve a positive return whatever the investment climate. To achieve this, hedge fund managers will use a variety of financial techniques – going short as in the take-over example, or simple hedging which means placing a bet to lock in a profit or avoid a loss on another bet.

The contrast is with a typical UK growth unit trust, which is compared with the stock market index, and where outperformance can mean that the fund falls 10% while the stock market falls 20%. A hedge fund manager would regard this 10% fall as a setback; he is looking all the time for growth.

How Hedge Funds Work

Hedge funds have been around for a number of years, but they really took off after the market setback of 2000–3. People began to realise that successful investment required active management – a team of researchers and analysts that only a financial organisation could afford. And that market setback cut deep: if you bought a typical portfolio of shares at the end of 1999, you would still be out of pocket nine years later.

The first feature you will notice about a hedge fund is the high minimum investment; the figures have come down over recent years but you will have to look hard to find a minimum as low as £5,000. The second feature you will notice is the fee structure: like an ordinary unit trust the hedge fund will charge you, say an initial 5% and 1% a year.

But the hedge fund will also charge you a performance fee, typically 20% of the extent to which it exceeds a pre-determined target, which can be defined as any positive return. Suppose your fund shares grow over target by 11%; performance fees will be based on 10%, allowing for the 1% management charge. The hedge fund manager will then take 20% of this 10%, which amounts to 2%, so that you will be left with 8% out of the original 11%. Your manager has taken much more than someone running a traditional unit trust.

How Long Do You Invest For?

- Up to a week: use spread-betting – no stamp duty, no CGT on profits (but also no tax offset for losses).

- A week to three months: use contracts for difference (CFDs) – the gearing, or leverage, magnifies your profits when you get it right; you do not pay stamp duty, but you do pay interest on the 90% or 95% of the position which you have effectively borrowed.

- Three months or longer: use shares.

Example: Contracts For Difference (CFDs)

John Rorke is convinced that Wizbang shares are due for a big rise over the next few weeks. The shares are quoted at 130/131p, so he buys 20,000 at 131p – as a CFD. If John had bought them as shares, they would have cost him nearly £30,000 including stamp duty. Instead, John has to put up a deposit of only 5% plus commission, which together costs him less than £1,500.

John is half-right: the shares do rise after only four weeks but just to 141/142p, so he sells out at 141p for his 20,000. His profit is 10p a share, equal to £2,000 less commission, though he also has to pay interest – for funding the cost of the 95% of his position, which the CFD provider effectively loaned to him.

Do's and Don'ts In The Stock Market

One of the most successful unit trust managers in the City of London, recently retired, jotted down six suggested rules to help you do well in the stock market.

- DON'T follow the crowd. The great dotcom. boom cost a lot of people a lot of money in both London and New York. You can make money by following fashionable investment – provided always you know when to get out!

▶

- DON'T let your ego get in the way of your business. You may be known as the guru in gold shares, but if they get too high, sell out, and become a guru in something else.
- DON'T throw good money after bad. Too many people take their profits and let their losses run, hoping that things will recover. Better to do the opposite – cut your losses and let your profits run.
- DO consider the most probable outcome, rather than focus on the best/worst case. This may explain why people take out life cover rather than critical illness or unemployment insurance, which are statistically more likely.
- DO look over the effective life of an investment rather than concentrate on the present. If people thought of themselves as an investment, more of them would start pension schemes early.
- DO admit to a mistake, swallow the loss and move on. Later, it may prove not to have been a mistake, but accept that you are not going to be right 100% of the time: 51% is fine.

Ways Into Hedge Funds

One way to invest in hedge funds is to buy shares in the management groups: the largest UK group is listed and others appear on AIM (Alternative Investment Market). An alternative is the 'fund-of-funds' route, which has been sponsored by some of the banks – these spread the risk but necessarily add to the cost.

These 'funds of alternative funds' are probably the most appealing way for individual investors to access hedge funds skills – not least because hedge funds are risky, as demonstrated by some spectacular crashes in the USA. Looking further ahead, we will probably see traditional type unit and investment trusts putting part of their assets into hedge funds.

Hedge funds have grown so fast over the last few years, producing positive returns in sagging stock markets, that they now form an important part of the investment scene. One key question remains: how will they perform when stock markets are rising – will they then be able to beat the low-cost trackers?

Or Does Private Equity Appeal?

Private equity is the buzzword in financial markets: well-known businesses such as Boots and the AA have been bought by private equity groups, and the Government of China has bought an interest in one of the leading US private equity companies.

Private equity lives up to its name: investing in assets which are private, not listed on the stock exchange. In some ways, private equity is the same sort of operation, on a larger scale, as Venture Capital Trusts and Enterprise Investment Schemes.

Cynics will tell you that private equity depends on cheap debt and rising share prices. The cheap debt is needed to finance take-overs: private equity bidders use maximum amounts of debt to make their offers, and will often take maximum borrowings on the assets of the companies they acquire. Rising share prices mean that the companies which have been bought can be restructured and floated again on the stock exchange.

Look At The Record

Private equity is more than the current buzzword: the record overall is good. Some private equity bids have failed and some re-flotations have been disappointing, but the consistent returns from good managers make this an interesting investment. Just because private equity is private, and independent of the stock market, it also represents a way of diversifying risk – a leading firm of advisers suggests that pension funds have at least 10% exposure to private equity.

These arguments make sense, too, for individual investors – and there is a simple and low-cost way to access private equity. This is through a group of around a dozen private equity investment trusts, whose shares can be bought in the stock market with the usual low minimum amounts.

There are two sorts of private equity investment trust – some invest direct in unquoted companies while others operate as fund-of-funds, with a portfolio of other investment trusts and private equity funds. Some trusts specialise in particular industries while some concentrate on particular regions.

Private equity investment trusts have performed well over recent years; though many people expect the rate of growth to slow down, a mixture of these funds (you can tailor the shares to your own taste) is well worth thinking about. One word of caution: private equity is not a fast performer, and if you buy into investment trusts you should be prepared to take a medium-term view.

Perks For Shareholders

Many UK companies offer perks to their shareholders in the form of benefits or discounts. Every investment expert will advise you, rightly, to look at the business' financial strength and not be distracted by side-benefits. But some companies will give you perks if you hold only one share, making them cost-effective – four of the best-known are shown in the list below.

Two words of caution:

- You may miss out if your shares are held through a nominee rather than owned direct, and;
- Some companies require that you are on the register for a minimum period, or that you are registered at a certain date.

▶

Marks & Spencer: Discount vouchers with the annual report, normally sent out around July.

Millennium & Copthorne: Discount vouchers for the company's hotels in the UK and Europe.

Moss Bros: Voucher for a 20% one-off discount on full price purchases at certain stores.

Signet: 10% discount on goods and services at this major jewellery group (includes H Samuel) – some watches excluded.

Companies offering perks if you hold a small number of shares include Eurotunnel, which offers discounts on cross-Channel car journeys – but check after the recent reorganisation. Landround offers hotel and travel discounts; Wolverhampton & Dudley gives a discount on food and accommodation.

Investing With Ethics

But hedge funds and private equity may not be for you – you may prefer to make ethically based decisions when you buy shares and bonds, in socially responsible investment (SRI). Nowadays, there are around 30 fund management groups that offer ethical funds, while for an ISA investor there are reckoned to be about 90 possible choices.

Ethical investment has grown dramatically since the first ethical funds were launched 20 years ago. Initially, there were fears that ethical funds would perform less well than average just because they were excluding major companies in drink, tobacco and armaments. But ethical funds have kept up with the mainstream; the FTSE4Good index, launched in 2001, has moved closely in line with the main stock market.

Dark and Light Green

One intriguing investment feature is that companies that score well on SRI tend to perform well in general: there seems to be a positive link between corporate social performance and financial performance. SRI started by excluding some sectors, such as drink and tobacco, but has now moved on to shades of green. Dark green funds use the strictest investment criteria; light green funds use a positive approach, by looking for companies that show improvements in their environmental or social policies.

If you invest in an ethical fund, you should follow the general rules for buying unit trusts; if you go to a financial adviser, you should readily be able to find one who specialises in ethical investment. Some banks and building societies also offer improved terms for loans on eco-friendly houses or for energy efficient investment.

You can invest direct in companies which feature in SRI. For example, you may be attracted by companies which make electric vehicles, specialise in solar power or have moved into producing biofuels. But be aware that they are often small (listed on AIM) and therefore that much riskier. And in ethical investment, as in other types, do not just follow fashion.

Make Money Grow On Trees!

The ultimate ecologically sound investment has to be to put money into trees. Investing in forestry can make good financial sense: forestry is a long-standing sustainable activity, which can appeal to people who are looking to the longer term and are prepared to commit part of a portfolio which they will not need to cash in at short notice.

There are two ways to invest in forestry – buy a part of a forest direct or invest in a forestry fund. Both routes bring the same significant tax advantages, which are:

1. After two years, your investment will no longer count as part of your estate for IHT, thanks to business property relief, and;
2. If you decide to sell your forestry investment during your lifetime, your profit from the timber will be free from CGT.

And if you receive income from your investment – though this may be more problematic – that will come to you free of tax.

Which route you follow, direct or a fund, is a matter of taste. Some people like to buy a forest, or part of one, and visit every summer. If you prefer an indirect stake, then the fund route will appeal – though in such a specialist area you may find charges are higher than on bond and share funds.

Forestry is a low-risk investment and there is now the possible chance of price appreciation as investors move in for a mix of financial and environmental reasons. Dermand from India and China is pushing up timber prices

Take Advice – or Go It Alone?

The fundamental question: do you manage your investments yourself, or do you go to an adviser? The DIY group have some knowledge, an interest in the financial area and the self-discipline needed to set aside the time. People who go to an adviser will be busy, maybe travelling a good deal or spending all hours running their own business – or maybe they believe in using specialist professional skills that are subject to outside supervision. If you go to an adviser, you will have to pay.

Many people choose to pay for advice: most of advisers' income comes from commission, which raises an immediate issue: advisers may be tempted to sell products that pay them the highest commission, even if these are not the best on the market and most suitable for their client. Fees are charged at around £200 an hour.

Three Grades of Adviser

So, how do you choose an adviser? The best guide is a personal recommendation to you from a satisfied customer. Unless you have that good fortune, you have to face up to the present structure – which the FSA is in process of changing yet again! There are three grades of financial adviser:

Independent Advisers: these cover the whole market, and give you the option of paying by fee or commission (in bigger deals, people tend to go for fees). In future, the FSA plans to emphasise qualifications and require independent advisers to work on a fee basis.

Tied Agents: they can advise only on the products of one financial supplier – they are often the sales staff of a bank or building society. Under the FSA's plans, tied agents will offer 'primary advice' at lower cost on simpler products. Their general aim is to separate the price for the product from the price for advice.

Multi-tied Agents: they can recommend the products of a limited selection of financial providers. They are to be known as general financial advisers – paid by commission, but no longer known as 'independent.'

How Do You Choose?

So you have talked to your friends, who have given you the names of three or four financial advisers. How do you choose someone to look after your hard-earned funds?

Ask Why? Before you go ahead, you need to formulate precisely why you are going to an adviser, and in which specific areas you are looking for advice. You may have some basic requirements, such as the wish to pursue an ethical investment policy – or you may be looking for advice in a particular sector, such as pensions.

Ask Where? Do you want to meet an adviser near your home or your office?

Ask Who? Do you prefer to take advice from a man or a woman?

Ask Qualifications? Probably the best overall guide to the service you are likely to get. Every adviser needs a financial planning certificate, but some move to certified or chartered financial planner status.

Ask How Much? You need to see a menu of charges, especially if you are paying fees that will be offset by commission which the adviser will keep.

Advice often seems to work best when people ask the adviser to review a portfolio which is not performing.

You get an assessment, which could well be free, plus a small annual commission for the adviser to keep your funds under review. If the upfront commission is high, the adviser has little incentive to provide long-term service; advisers who are paid annually are more likely to look after you in the long term.

Summary
♦ You can make significant profits by buying shares in companies that are taken over – buy after a bid has failed, where another company holds a stake or after a bid has been announced. Invest in a 'special situations' unit trust.

♦ Through spread-betting you can back your judgement that a share price is going to rise or fall; you do not have to put up a big stake. Contracts for difference (CFDs) are widely used in short-term dealing; you borrow, at a cost, but this magnifies your gain if you get it right.

♦ Hedge funds aim to make money whatever the state of the stock market. The initial investment may have to be large, and the manager will typically want 20% of the amount by which he beats an agreed index. Consider a fund-of-funds way in.

♦ Private equity firms have taken over major companies and made big profits. You can share through investment trusts which invest direct or operate as fund-of-funds.

- Ethical investment has become popular, with nearly 100 unit trusts available;
  you can invest direct, but the companies tend to be small and therefore risky. Think about forestry (direct or through a fund) if you have assets you do not need to keep liquid.

- Think carefully whether you want to do your own investing or whether to go to an adviser. Decide just what you want from an adviser, and spend time choosing them; look at their qualifications.

Chapter 8

The Seventh Way – Save On Pensions

Pensions have had a bad press over the last few years. This has made people forget their two great advantages – that you can offset your pension contributions against tax, and that you can take 25% of your pension fund, in cash, free of tax.

Property has become a popular pension asset since the late 1990s, when Gordon Brown hit pension funds a severe blow by disallowing dividend credits. The stock market crashed in 2000–03 and annuity rates fell because we are all living longer.

The answer has to be – spread your risk, take out a pension and also invest in shares and property. Pensions should form part of your retirement fund because the combination of tax relief and 25% tax-free cash gives strikingly high returns.

John Steel Made a Pension Contribution and Earned 15%!

John Steel, age 65, is an IT manager who pays tax in the 40% bracket. He is due to retire under his employer's (now discontinued) final salary scheme but he would like to add a pension of his own. This is what he does, step by step:

1. He cashes in ISAs to give him £20,000, which he puts into a pension policy. He gets tax relief at 40%, which amounts to £8,000, so that the net cost of his policy has come down to £12,000.
2. He then cashes in 25% of his policy as the rules allow. Two things happen: he pockets £5,000 free of tax, and the policy is reduced by the same amount to £15,000 from £20,000.
3. John pauses at this point to see just where he has got to: he has a policy for £15,000 which has cost him £7,000, or less than half its face value. He paid out £20,000 to start with, but he got back £8,000 in tax relief and £5,000 from cashing in 25%.
4. That looks good, but where does he stand on income? John decides to put the money into an annuity – as most people do. He discusses this with his wife Gwen, and they both decide to go for the largest immediate income. This means choosing a level annuity, which is fixed in money terms. It also means choosing an annuity for John alone – a 'single life'; Gwen will be protected by the widow's benefit in John's employer's pension scheme.
5. So John goes into the marketplace with his £15,000 policy: he goes to a broker and also looks on the internet. One of the leading insurance companies offers him 7.19%, which will give John an annual income of just over £1,000.

6. This policy cost John £7,000. He does the sum: his precise annual income is £1,078, which is equal to 15.4% on his outlay. This is three times the rate John is getting on his deposit account – Gwen is convinced she married a financial wizard.

And It Still Works At Standard Rate!

John rushes round to tell all his friends how to earn 15.4%. His contemporary, Bill, works for another company, but his salary is smaller than John's so that he pays tax at the standard rate of 20%. John and Bill sit down and do the sums.

Bill would only want to put in £10,000 into a pension fund, on which his tax relief would be £2,000. His pension would then cost him £8,000 and he would cash in 25%, as John did. Bill would then have a policy of £7,500, which would have cost him £5,500 – so still looking good.

Bill has not yet approached an insurance company, but he takes John's rate of 7.19%: they are the same age with similar health histories. On a policy of £7,500, that would give Bill an annual income of just under £540. Working out the precise figures and relating his income to the policy cost of £5,500, Bill reckons that he will earn 9.8%. That is nearly double what as he gets from a bank deposit – so Bill too goes ahead.

Add a Tax-efficient Stakeholder

The Steel family have another tax-saving pension benefit: Gwen, John's wife, has a stakeholder pension. Some years ago, Gwen's father, who is a retired bank manager, phoned and asked if she would like a stakeholder pension. Gwen pointed out that she did not have an income – and how could someone else give her a pension? No problem, her father replied.

Her father explained that stakeholder pensions were set up back in 2001 to encourage savings – so charges are low, minimum contributions are small and you are free to stop, re-start or move your plan. But the new feature of stakeholders was that you did not need an income to contribute towards a pension. And someone else could arrange a stakeholder pension for you – some people set them up for their children.

With a Subsidy From The Chancellor

Gwen's father goes on to explain how you can acquire £1,000 of pension assets for £800 – thanks to help from the Chancellor. You can invest up to £3,600 a year, but you get relief at the 20% standard rate of tax. This means that you only have to send the insurance company £2,880 and the other £720 is added by the Revenue. (Gwen's father points out that the cut in standard rate of tax to 20% from 22% has made stakeholders a little less attractive.)

Stakeholder pensions are open to most UK residents
– the main exclusions being controlling directors of
companies and higher-paid executives who are members
of a company pension scheme. A stakeholder works just
like any other pension plan: you can take your pension
any time after age 50 (going up to 55 in 2010), when
you can turn 25% into cash. By age 75 you must turn
the pension into an annuity or an Alternatively Secured
Pension (see later in this chapter).

Example: Gain From A Stakeholder

Gwen's father took out the stakeholder pension
for her seven years ago, getting a policy worth
£3,600 a year at a cost of £2,880, so that over the
seven years the immediate subsidy has reached a
useful £5,040. He found little advertising – the
sponsors' profit margins are relatively slender. He
used the internet and found an insurance company
which charged less than the permitted maximum.

When the policy is cashed in, the average
annual return over the seven years emerges at
6% – Gwen's father deliberately played it safe.
This means that Gwen has a pension fund worth
£30,000, which has cost £20,000 over the seven
years: the combination of a subsidised pension
policy and moderate investment growth have
netted the family £10,000, equal to a 50% return
on the money invested. Gwen thinks her father is
a financial wizard.

How To Use a Stakeholder

Taking a cue from this example, you can see that it would also make sense for a husband to take out a stakeholder plan for his partner if she has no or only a small income – at home looking after young children. The facility to start, stop and transfer your plan makes the operations simple, and enables you to move to another company if you find performance is disappointing.

You could take out stakeholder pension plans for your children – especially useful if the policies are financed by grandparents. The snag is that your children cannot retire before age 50, soon rising to 55, unless they become professional athletes. Some grandparents have found stakeholders a useful way to reduce IHT (a regular payment out of income which does not affect their standard of living) and perhaps run the scheme for five or seven years.

Two Crucial Dates For Your Pension

Two dates are important in your pension strategy: one is when you retire, which will be 60 or 65 for many people; the second is age 75 when you are compelled by legislation to make certain decisions.

Many people who retire at, say, age 65 will take out an annuity. But there are alternatives worth considering.

Income Drawdown

The first option for a 65-year-old retiree is income drawdown – though this is suitable only for larger pension funds. Instead of using your pension investments to buy an annuity, you draw an income while your fund stays invested. There are rules: the maximum income you can draw is about 120% of a level lifetime annuity, the minimum income you can draw is nil.

People who have a large fund, and especially those with investment skills, can choose to leave their fund invested and draw no income. If you retire at 65 you have 10 years before the rules start to bite at age 75; if you are skilful or lucky, you will then have a bigger fund with which to buy your annuity. (You can generally switch your fund into an annuity at any time you choose.)

This is a moderately risky policy, which is why income drawdown is best suited to large funds. There is another risk: if you take the maximum permitted income and your portfolio does not perform. In that case, you will have sacrificed capital in order to maintain income, which is why you need a cushion in the shape of a substantial portfolio.

Phased Retirement

There is a half-way house between putting all your pension fund into an annuity and income drawdown, where your fund stays invested and you draw maybe no income at all. This half-way house is phased retirement, where you buy annuities but spread the buying over, say, five years.

The way it works is straightforward: in the first year you put one-fifth of your fund into an annuity, so that your income for that year consists of the 25% tax free cash plus the annuity you have bought. You can plan to make larger annuity purchases in the earlier years, so that your tax-free cash receipts will decline while the annuity payments increase. Your ability to arrange this sort of fine-tuning forms one of the attractions of phased retirement plans.

Phased retirement can be especially useful for people who move from full-time to part-time work rather than going immediately into retirement. And as part of your fund remains invested, you will still have some scope to exercise your investment skills. Your personal financial position will dictate how many years you decide to phase, and particularly when you start.

Example: A Pension At Less Than Half Price
Jack Gimblett, 59, is financial consultant to a Cambridge IT company. He gets an annual fee of £60,000 and this year is given a £30,000 bonus for helping on the management buy-out. Jack thinks it's time to do something about his pension.

▶

He cashes in ISAs to put in £20,000; he goes to the bank and borrows another £20,000. He puts the £40,000 into a pension plan; as Jack is a higher-rate taxpayer he gets relief of £16,000. He does not take any income (he uses income drawdown with nil pension) but cashes in the permitted 25% of his fund, which gives him a £10,000 lump sum.

Jack is now £26,000 better off, so he repays the £20,000 bank loan and pockets the surplus £6,000. He has a pension fund worth £30,000 (after taking the 25% in cash), which has cost him just £14,000 – the original £20,000 he put in, less the £6,000 surplus.

But one of Jack's friends is worried: the Revenue drew up anti-avoidance rules to prevent 're-cycling' the tax-free lump sum in pensions. Jack knows the answer: the anti-avoidance rules do not apply so long as the lump sum is no more than 1% of the lifetime pension allowance – and that 1% amounted to £16,000 for 2007–8 and £16,500 for 2008–9.

Jack has got his pension fund at less than half price!

Now You're 75

When you reach age 75, your choices become restricted. You have to buy a lifetime annuity or an Alternatively Secured Pension (ASP), which was introduced a few years ago to provide an option to an annuity.

An ASP works rather like Income Drawdown:

- Maximum income is limited to around 70% of a comparable annuity, the limit being reviewed annually;

- Maximum income will be based on age 75 whatever your actual age – so as you get older, you will do relatively worse. As in Income Drawdown, you can switch to a lifetime annuity at any time.

You Can Leave a Pension – But Not Capital

Two years ago, the Revenue moved the goal posts on ASPs. You have to draw at least 55% of the comparable annuity rate, which limits your ability to build up funds. When the ASP member dies, any assets which remain can only be used to pay dependants' pensions or be given to a charity free of tax. Any other payment will face a swingeing tax charge of up to 70%; as ASP assets are also subject to IHT, the total tax bill could reach a staggering 80+%. An ASP remains the only alternative to buying an annuity at age 75 – but on these terms it seems unlikely to find many takers.

Your estate will escape IHT when remaining ASP funds are used to buy pensions for your beneficiaries – but there is a catch. If your beneficiary dies and some of your ASP funds still remain, then those funds will be caught for IHT.

Conventional Annuities

Annuities are called conventional because about 90% of people buy them when they retire. An annuity provides income in return for a capital payment and that income comes with virtually total security.

But this security, which has wide appeal, commands a price. That price is lack of flexibility: once you have bought an annuity you will not be able to change it, cash it in, or transfer it; you probably will not be able to borrow on it. The moral is simple: you need to think hard and carefully about what type of annuity you want.

How To Buy

The first important feature to take on board is the 'open market option'. Though you may have built up your pension fund with Insurance Co. X, you do not have to go to them for your annuity. To find the best rates, look at the weekend newspapers, which carry annuity data, or log on the internet; you can go to a broker, for which you will pay. Industry estimates suggest that you can do 10–15% better by shopping around than going to your existing insurer.

It can make sense, allowing for the cost, to use an intermediary; you should get some useful advice, and at least you will have someone to sue if things do go wrong!

Impaired Annuities

If you are one of the 22% of adults in Britain who smoke, you may qualify for improved annuity rates. The insurers' view is simple: if your smoking habits, or a history of illness or surgery, are likely to reduce your lifespan then you will get a better rate – possibly significantly better.

The guidelines in this area have to be widely drawn and rates relate very much to individual cases. The test for smokers is that you smoke 10 or more cigarettes a day and have done so for the past 10 years. Heart conditions, many types of cancer and major surgery can also give you an improved annuity rate.

If you think you come into this category, you need to take advice and you also need to allow extra time for the annuity to be agreed. You should speak to your doctor first – his evidence will be needed. Remember that the insurance company is not interested primarily in your current lifestyle but in the impact of your medical history on your life expectation.

Standard Annuities: The Choices

Never forget: when you take out an annuity, it is set in stone. So you need to take a decision on each aspect of your annuity; you need to be aware how your decisions will affect your annuity income and you will need to talk to your spouse or partner.

Your first choice directly involves your partner: do you want to arrange that, when you die, they will continue to receive an income for the rest of their life? You can arrange for your partner to receive 100%, i.e. the same amount as your own annuity. That is the most expensive option, and will be even more expensive if your partner is a good deal younger.

Most people opt for a partner's annuity in the 50–70% range, which will cost you a 10–15% income cut – compared with the position if you chose to have no partner's pension. There is no magic in the proportion you choose: people seem to have followed the limit set by the Revenue on company schemes, where the maximum widow's pension was set at two-thirds.

Coping With Inflation

Inflation is the enemy of pensioners – not just massive price rises of 10–15% a year, which happened during the 1970s. Even small annual increases over the years can reduce living standards.

Example: How Inflation Hurts

Jack Barnes retired at age 60 with a level annuity of £10,000 a year; he wanted to obtain the maximum level of current income.

The Bank of England keeps the annual rate of inflation to 2.5% but Jack realises that after 10 years his £10,000 is worth only £7,500. Many men, and most women, are expected to live to age 80; in Jack's case, the real value of his annuity would drop again, this time to less than £6,000.

This means that by age 80, at a moderate rate of inflation by recent standards, Jack will have lost more than 40% of the real value of his annuity.

To Escalate – or Not To Escalate?

Jack Barnes' problem, in the example just quoted, was that at age 60 he could not know how long he was going to live, nor what levels future inflation would reach. That is the problem facing everyone who buys an annuity: you have to make decisions on the basis of facts you cannot possibly know.

A present-day 60 year old, hearing Jack Barnes' story, could ask for an annuity whose payments escalate in line with the retail prices index (RPI). That would solve the problem of keeping up with inflation – at a price (and if prices were ever to fall, the annuity payments would also fall).

The price for an annuity linked to RPI is a heavy cost in terms of current income – a sacrifice of about one-third compared with a level annuity.

Example

Sid Barnes, who is Jack Barnes' nephew, reaches age 60 and, after his uncle's story, insists on a RPI-linked annuity. He is surprised to discover that instead of a level annuity of £10,000 a year, his RPI-linked payments come in at less than £7,000.

Still, Sid consoles himself that the payments will rise each year in line with inflation. But when he does the sums, he realises that it will take around 15 years (with inflation running at 2.5%) for his inflation-proofed annuity to reach the amount he could get today for a level annuity. He wonders what he should have done?

Best of Both Worlds?

If your great concern is inflation over the years ahead, and family history suggests you have a long life to come, then you should go for an RPI-linked annuity. The loss of income as against a level annuity is the price you are paying for security.

There is a compromise: instead of linking to the RPI, you could buy a fixed rate of annual increase – the larger the built-in increase, the more it will cost. You could ask say for 2% annual increases; these would cost you a 20% reduction in income compared with a level annuity, to around £8,000 a year against £10,000. And you can easily calculate that at that rate of increase, it will take just over 10 years to catch up to the figure for annual payments that a level annuity would give you today.

There is no simple answer to the Barnes family conundrum. Probably the most appealing solution is to take a level annuity, giving you the maximum income and set aside some of that income to put into tax-free investments. These should give you some protection against future inflation – and represent funds which you can access. Whichever annuity you choose, you have given up the ability to access your capital.

Do You Want a Guarantee Period?

Most companies that provide annuities will offer a guarantee period, generally five or 10 years. This means simply that the annuity will continue to be paid for the guarantee period even if you die within that time.

Guarantees are not expensive and are worth considering for your family's sake, if you were to die after a short retirement. If you have opted for a level annuity with no partner's pension then it makes good sense to choose a guarantee, probably of 10 years.

How Often Do You Want To Be Paid?

Most people ask to be paid monthly, probably because their salary was paid that way when they were working. There is not much difference – except when payments begin – between monthly in advance and monthly in arrears. Monthly in advance is probably the most popular, though monthly in arrears is fractionally cheaper.

Unlock Your Pension?

If your retirement age is 60 or 65, with no provision in the scheme for early retirement, and someone suggests that you should unlock your pension, that sounds like a good idea – or is it?

Pension unlocking works on the rule that anyone with a personal pension can retire at age 50 (rising to 55 in two years' time) and that when you retire you can cash in 25% and buy an annuity or go for income drawdown if the fund is big enough. Most people's pension comes from an occupational scheme set up by their employer; in that case, the pension fund has to be transferred out of the occupational scheme into a personal plan.

There are two snags: the first is that the transfer into a personal plan will cost you commission, which will be taken by your adviser. The second, and much more important, snag is that your annuity will not give you nearly as much as a company pension.

The FSA's Example

Jack Bowes, age 53, needs cash. His employer's human resources manager tells Jack that when he retires at 65 he will get a pension of £1,800 a year.

But Jack feels that he cannot wait that long, so he goes to a financial adviser to unlock his pension. He gets a cash lump sum of £4,300 – but his pension at 65 will now be only £340 a year. So, in exchange for the £4,300 cash now at age 53, Jack will be giving up nearly £1,500 a year from age 65 for the rest of his life.

By unlocking his pension, Jack is paying a heavy price for the ability to get his hands on £4,300 ready cash. What are his alternatives? Maybe equity release on his house, maybe careful switching of balance transfers on credit cards, maybe a bank loan; these will cost – but less than he will pay through unlocking his occupational pension, which he now sees should be a last resort.

You could, if you wish, arrange to be paid annually. In that case, there is a significant difference between payment in advance and payment in arrears. If you choose to be paid in arrears, annually or even six monthly, you need to take on board the question of 'proportion'.

Essentially, this protects your family if you die between payments (especially if you die just before the next payment is due), and is not particularly expensive. When you die, an annuity with proportion will pay an amount which is proportionate from the last payment up to the date of death.

SIPP: DIY Pensions

One of the welcome new freedoms introduced in 2006 was the SIPP: the self-invested pension fund. SIPPs are a type of personal pension which offer a wider choice of funds than standard personal pensions or company schemes and, since April 2006, SIPPs have been available to people who also want to keep paying into their company pension scheme – a wise choice when your employer also contributes.

SIPPs allow you to invest in shares, as well as financial instruments such as futures and options; most appealing for many people, they also allow you to invest in commercial property. Originally, residential property and buy-to-let were included, but Gordon

Brown back-tracked; you will not be allowed to put unquoted shares into a SIPP where you control the business. The only limit on SIPPs is the overall maximum for your pension contributions, i.e. your annual salary up to £235,000 for 2008–9.

SIPPs appeal to people looking for investment choice; a stakeholder would be a cheaper option if you are happy to stay with a conventional balanced fund. Though costs have come down, you should probably have a minimum of £20,000 to invest for a SIPP to be economic: some SIPP providers require a minimum investment, many charge a set-up fee and most also require an annual fee.

. . . and a Lump of Tax-free Cash

For many people, one of the blessings of retirement will be the ability to take 25% of your pension fund in cash – free of tax and available for any purpose you choose. (Some people who were members of a company pension scheme before April 2006 may be able to take even more: you should talk to your pensions manager and you may need expert advice.)

Pre-2006, you had to draw an income from your pension if you wanted to take tax-free cash. Since then, you have been free to take the cash and carry on working – but not all employers and insurance companies will permit this benefit.

The case for taking cash is almost irresistible: there will not be many other occasions when you receive a large tax-free sum and for higher-rate taxpayers the case is particularly strong. If you choose not to take the cash option, your pension will be maintained: otherwise, it would be reduced by one-third.

Example: Do You Take The Cash?

Alan Smailes will pay standard rate income tax when he retires on a pension of £6,000 a year. All his friends urge him to take £30,000 of tax-free cash (using the Revenue multiplier of 20X for the total fund) but Alan pauses.

He understands that his pension will be cut to two-thirds if he takes cash, but he does not have any pressing need for the money. He is more concerned about the size of the income difference and the benefit to his partner, who will get 67% of his pension when he dies. He calculates that after 10 years, if pensions rise 2.5% a year, he will be £2,000 a year better off than if he takes cash. If he dies around that time, his partner's pension will be just over £5,000 a year against just under £4,000 – and he knows these payments are risk-free.

Alan is one of the few who decide not to take retirement cash.

Women Get a Tough Pension Deal

Pensions are one of the major areas where women still do badly. Women earn on average less than men, they often take time out to look after young children and, as they live longer than men, they have a longer retirement to finance. According to official data, over two-thirds of women have failed to build up entitlement to the full state pension and more than 2 million women have not accrued any entitlement at all.

A few minor improvements are being made: the number of years' contributions for women to qualify for a full state pension is being cut to 30 from 39, and from 2010 tax credits for mothers and carers will be calculated weekly rather than annually so they can build up more qualifying years. Against this, the pension age is rising for both men and women: women born after April 1950 will not get a state pension until after the current retirement age of 60.

The moral has to be that women need to take early action to build up their pensions. Stakeholder pensions, which are flexible and accept small amounts, are especially useful – a low-cost stakeholder invested in tracker units has long-term appeal.

Summary
♦ **Pensions have two big advantages – your contributions are tax-deductible and you can**

take 25% cash. A higher-rate taxpayer who retires at 65 can make 15% on his money!

♦ Stakeholder pensions are cheap and flexible and they carry a Government subsidy. Anyone can invest up to £3,600 a year but you only have to pay £2,880; the Inland Revenue supplies the other £720.

♦ You can take an annuity at age 65, but you have two other options – income drawdown and phased retirement. Income drawdown is suited to larger pension pots; in phased retirement you spread your annuity buying over several years.

♦ At age 75, you have to buy an annuity or take an Alternatively Secured Pension (ASP). There are limits on the income you can draw from an ASP and you cannot leave capital tax-free to your family, just pensions.

♦ Nine out of ten people buy annuities. Pause before you buy, because an annuity cannot be changed once you have signed up. If you are a smoker, check if you can get better terms under an impaired annuity.

♦ Look on the internet or talk to a broker to get the best annuity rate. First big decision: do you want an annuity that is fixed in money – or do you want it inflation-proofed at the expense of current payments? Then: annuity on your life or also on your partner's? Guarantee period? How often do you want to be paid?

♦ SIPP: the self-invested pension plan, the DIY of the pension world. This will cost you rather more than a stakeholder scheme, but you will be able to make your own investment decisions, e.g. to buy into commercial property.

♦ Women have a hard deal on pensions: they earn less than men and live longer. So women need to act early – especially as their state pension is being deferred.

Chapter 9

And Paying For Uni – Plus other Family Bills

Great news! Young Jack or Jill has won a place at university, which will improve their minds and should get them better jobs. That just leaves you, the proud parents, to reflect on how to pay for it all.

You need to get your mind round one number:

- There will be a shortfall, of at least £15,000–£20,000 and maybe a good deal more, between the maximum student loans and the total cost of their going to university.

You and the soon-to-be undergraduates next need to look at the loan possibilities (all figures are for 2008–9 and should rise roughly in line with inflation):

- Maximum loans for students at London universities, and living away from home, are £6,475. A quarter of this amount will be means-tested on the basis of household income, so some students will be eligible for only 75% of the maximum figure.

- Loans for fees offer up to £3,070 per year, which the Student Loans Company will pay direct to the university. The fees can be paid upfront, if you choose.

- Maintenance grants of £2,765 – the full grant – will be available when household earnings amount to less than £17,910. Households where earnings are between £17,911 and £38,330 will receive a partial grant. Incomes above £38,330 receive no grant.

- Bursaries of a minimum £300 a year are for students who receive the full maintenance grant and are charged the maximum fee of £3,070 a year.

Example

Bill Johnston, who is a first year student at Cambridge, did not bother to apply for a student loan – his father runs a hedge fund in the City and is well-off. But Johnston senior explains to Bill that he is missing a trick.

The maximum maintenance loan he could have is £4,510, of which one-quarter is means-tested. This means that young Bill could draw a loan of three-quarters of that, which amounts to £3,382. The rate of interest, which is fixed for a year at a time, is currently 4.8%; it will rise in line with inflation.

▶

Bill does the sum: if he draws the loan and invests in a three-year deposit he will make a turn on the interest – as his father might say – of around £250. As Bill does not have any other income, this £250 will be tax-free as it is well covered by his personal allowance. Bill is a chip off the old block!

Banks Bearing Gifts

Cinema tickets, rail passes, discounts on books, CDs, gigs – these are just a few of the offers facing Jack or Jill from high street banks. You, or they, need to step back: what a student wants is an interest-free overdraft which will last the whole of the university course. When this was written, two major banks were offering interest-free overdrafts in the £2,500–£3,000 range; other banks offered rather smaller amounts, and these were often stepped – say £1,000 to first-year students, £1,250 for second year and up to £1,500 for final year.

So your first job is to make sure that the new student chooses an interest-free overdraft. Your second job is to see that they apply straightaway to the bank to take advantage of the interest-free borrowing: a letter from the university should be enough.

When all this has been done, think about freebies. If the new student will be using the train, think about the free five-year Young Person's Railcard offered by one bank.

Need a Bigger Overdraft?

There is a fundamental rule in dealing with banks: if you think you may need to borrow more, contact them in advance. Do not just use funds beyond your overdraft or break an agreed finance limit.

This rule applies especially to students: authorised borrowing rates typically range between 7% and 10%, but the penalty for unauthorised borrowing can now (subject to the High Court) reach up to £30 a day! If you go beyond your overdraft by accident, contact the bank at once and see if they will drop the penalty charges.

Buy Them a House!

Parents are buying student flats and houses for their children – for many people, this is the first step into the world of buy-to-let. Buying your student children a property takes care of a major outlay; student properties tend not to be expensive and your investment will benefit from a rise in UK house prices.

If you buy the property, you will have to pay tax on rental income when rooms are let to other students. You will also have to face a CGT bill when you come to sell, on similar lines to a second home.

One answer is to buy the property in your child's name. They could then benefit from Rent-a-Room relief, when the first £4,250 of rental income each year is free of tax. If they do have to pay tax on rents, the chances are that they will be able to use their full allowances and end up paying no tax or only 20%. (To be safe, make sure that you live for another seven years in case the taxman argues that the house was a potentially-exempt gift.)

Example: Rent-a-Room Relief

Sam Loxton is a second-year student at Sheffield where his father has bought a four-bedroom house. Sam lets out three rooms, which bring in £160 a week, totalling £5,500 over the university year; Sam has other income, as he works in his father's textile factory during vacations.

He can offset expenses against the rental income from the three rooms – council tax, insurance, water, gas and electricity and he gets an allowance for the wear and tear of furniture and furnishings. Sam reckons that he can offset £2,900 in this way so that he will have to pay tax on £2,600.

But he realises that he would be better off to claim Rent-a-Room relief. This scheme allows rent up to £4,250 to be tax-free when it arises

from letting out furnished accommodation in your
main home. (You do not have to be the owner;
but you have to be living in the property, and the
scheme does not apply to rooms let as offices.)
When Sam claims this relief, he will pay tax on
the amount by which his rental income exceeds
£4,250 – i.e. £1,250.

Sam has halved his tax liability!

. . . and Save CGT

When you buy the property in your child's name,
it will then count as their main home ('principal
residence') and so free from CGT when it is sold. But
the relief will be less than 100% because they have
been letting out rooms: the basis is pro-rata, so that if
you bought a four-bedroom house and two rooms were
let, then your son or daughter could claim 50% relief.

If you feel that you want to keep the property in your
own name, you can still cope with tax on rents. You
can enter into a formal agreement with your child,
splitting ownership, say 90-10, but allocating all the
rental income to your child. They may have to pay tax,
but the bill will be much less than if all the rent went
to you. You can reduce the CGT bill as you would on a
second home, by registering it as your principal private
residence for a short period, which will make the last
three years free from CGT when you sell.

Example: Buying a Student House

Richard Hutton's daughter, Susan, has won a place at Edinburgh University to read French and Spanish; Richard and his wife plan to buy her a student house where she can let rooms. Richard checks on a survey by Landlord Mortgages, the broker, and finds that Edinburgh is dearer than London or Oxbridge – a student house will cost around £300,000. As he is buying on a mortgage, the price means that interest will be bigger than the rental income, and Richard plans on a shortfall of £15,000 over three years.

The big plus is the prospect of capital gains: a price rise of 5% a year would give a profit of £45,000 at the end of the three years. Richard would have to pay CGT if he owned the house, so it goes to Susan where it becomes her principal residence.

Susan's second choice was Nottingham, where the economics could not be more different. A student house would cost about £80,000, and the rent would give a surplus over mortgage interest of around £10,000. But the capital gain would be smaller, at £10,000–£15,000. If Susan had gone to Nottingham, Richard would have kept the house in his own name and his wife's and arranged for most of the rent to go to Susan. The tipping-point for a student house is around £150,000: if you pay less, the rent will cover the mortgage interest – if you pay more, there will be an income shortfall but the capital gain should be bigger.

You Need To Take Cover

Insurance issues may not feature among the new student's priorities – but they should: laptops and mobiles cost money. The best solution is to arrange stand-alone insurance; some parents extend their home insurance, but as a rule this is probably not a good idea. You need to check the small print, to make sure that the policy covers belongings away from home and that your son or daughter can comply with any security requirements. If you like this idea, remember that any claims the student makes will affect your no-claim bonus.

If the new student goes into university accommodation, such as a hall of residence, check to see whether the fees include insurance cover. In a shared house, think about insurance which is offered by several of the major banks as part of their package deals for students. There are also specialist companies which offer insurance for students, which are most easily accessed at the university.

Payback Time

Repayment of student loans begins in the April after graduation, taken through the PAYE system at the rate of 9% of earnings above £15,000. You can make overpayments, but the rate on student loans is so low that it hardly makes financial sense to accelerate the payback.

How To Manage Family Finance

When you start a relationship, and above all when you enter a family situation, you need to look on the dark side – you may die, you may be hurt in an accident or you may fall ill.

You need to make a will, and to do that you should go to a solicitor. Making a will is essential if you are in a heterosexual partnership (i.e. not married or in a civil partnership) and strongly desirable if you are not. Nowadays, the costs are not heavy. The first purpose of a will is to direct where your assets go; remember that in a heterosexual partnership your partner has no rights unless they can show that they were financially dependent. In England remember that there is no such thing as a 'common law marriage'. (The rules for wills are the same in England and Wales, slightly different in Northern Ireland and very different in Scotland.)

Hard Deal For Widows

If you are married with young children, your widow (or widower) will get a far from generous deal unless you make a will. Under the law of intestacy she will get £125,000, personal assets and income from 50% of the rest: the children get 50% when they reach age 18 and the other 50% when their surviving parent dies.

Above all, if you want to save inheritance tax when you are not married or in a civil partnership by using the £312,000 nil rate band and saving the family

£125,000, you need to make a will. And when you make a will you need to appoint an executor, whose job is to collect the estate and distribute it according to the rules.

Review Your Will Every Five Years

You can appoint a friend (preferably younger than you) who can also be a beneficiary; alternatively, use the firm of solicitors who drew up the will. Keep your will in a safe place, such as with your bank or the solicitors, and review it, say, every five years: people, their assets and tax laws all change.

Remember that, in general, marriage or remarriage will revoke a will you have made. You can always change your will by adding a codicil or, probably better, setting up a new will.

Suppose You Are Only Injured?

You may die early – before the average which is now 79 for men and 84 for women. But there is a greater chance that you will be hurt or injured, in a car smash or a domestic accident. To deal with this possibility, you need a power of attorney.

A power of attorney is essentially simple: it enables person B to act on behalf of person A in various sorts of financial affairs and even make health and welfare decisions for them. (Scottish rules and terminology are different from those in England and Wales.)

You probably gave a solicitor a power of attorney to complete the purchase of your flat; you probably exchanged general powers of attorney with your partner so that you could cash a cheque or take up a share offer. Power of attorney can be limited in time or related to specific events.

This ordinary power of attorney will work fine if you are abroad or on holiday and you want someone else to handle a deal that cannot wait; you will probably send copies to your bank or company registrar. If there is no time limit, you can always cancel the power of attorney through a simple deed of revocation.

But If It's Worse?

So, an ordinary power of attorney will work perfectly well if, say, you are laid up in a Spanish hospital with a broken leg. But it will not work if you are laid up in that hospital with concussion and in a coma.

Formally, your ordinary power of attorney will be revoked automatically if you, the donor, 'lose mental capacity'. This is just when you most need the power of attorney, but you cannot create one and your existing one is ended.

Enduring/Lasting Power of Attorney

The title says it: this type allows someone to look after your property and financial affairs if you become unable to do so at some stage in the future. When the attorney believes that you are becoming mentally incapable, they have to register. You can draw up an enduring power of attorney which will come into action when you lose your mental capacity – say suddenly in a major car accident.

Since October 2007, the Enduring Power of Attorney (EPA) has been replaced by the Lasting Power of Attorney (LPA), but un-registered EPAs can still be registered. The new LPA allows other people to look after your health affairs, as well as property and finance – an LPA is more cumbersome and costs more than the old EPA.

The legal system will cope even if you do not have an EPA/LPA, but the procedure is time-consuming and expensive. An application has to be made to the Court of Protection, and your family will have no say in deciding who looks after your affairs: the Court will choose.

If You're an Attorney?

In a moment of generosity, you may have agreed to act as attorney for a colleague. They then crash their car and lie in a coma. You have to register the power of attorney with the Public Guardianship Office and you have to tell your colleague's close relatives – they can object if they choose. You will get a properly sealed document, for which you will pay a fee. Your mission statement: you must act in the best interests of your unlucky colleague at all times.

Cover Against a Critical Illness

Protecting yourself and your family comes down to probabilities – and critical illness is more likely (or less unlikely) than ending up in a coma after a car crash. Critical illness is generally reckoned to cover six conditions: cancer, heart attack, bypass surgery, kidney failure, organ transplant and stroke. Whether you choose this type of insurance will depend partly on family history.

If you are employed, your first step should be to establish whether the company offers protection if you contract a critical illness and are unable to work. If you are self-employed, you probably need to talk to a specialist financial adviser. This is a complex area for you to make the decisions and if you take advice you will have the right to complain and possibly get compensation if you end up with the wrong policy.

New guidelines from the Association of British Insurers should help people making claims for critical illness, payment protection and life insurance. Where policy holders did not disclose all the details, insurers must now pay in full if the non-disclosure was accidental or irrelevant. Even when the policy holder was negligent, the ABI says that the claim should still be paid in part. Only when non-disclosure was deliberate should claims be denied in full.

Assuming you choose critical illness insurance, and have to buy it yourself, there is one basic rule: tell all about any past health problems. You will get a 'keyfacts' document when you buy insurance, which in critical illness you will read carefully – but unless you are an expert, go for outside specialist help.

Protecting Your Income

To sum up so far: you have basic life cover – say up to four times your salary if you are employed, and if you are self-employed you and your partner have taken your own insurance. You may have critical illness cover, but you appreciate there is a more basic problem: what if you can't work because of a non-critical illness?

This is the key protection issue facing many people, and is much more probable than death, disabling injury or critical illness. If you are employed, you need to establish what would be available. If you are self-employed, or employed but unhappy at what would be available, then you need to look at Income Protection.

How Long To Defer

An Income Protection policy will cover you for a fixed amount of money or a proportion of your earnings. Income Protection policies pay out only after an agreed period; the differences in cost depend largely on how long you are prepared to make this deferred period: you could choose a month, or a year or more. The longer the period, the lower the premium. The payout will be based on your earnings over the previous twelve months.

One important point to watch is just when the policy would pay out – when you cannot do your own job or when you cannot do any job. Being unable to do your own job is better cover but more difficult to find.

Cover Your Mortgage . . .

There is another way to approach protection – decide which is your principal liability, and cover that. For many people, their biggest single commitment is their mortgage, so it could make sense to take out mortgage payment protection insurance (MPPI), especially as for newer mortgages the state will not help for the first nine months you are unemployed or disabled.

Terms vary among companies, so you need to read the small print or get expert help. You can get cover for accidents, illness and unemployment or just one of those. The basic decision is how long you want benefits to run: one year or more. The longer the benefit period, the more the policy will cost.

For unemployment cover there is often an initial exclusion period at the start of the contract – 30 or 60 days – during which you may not claim. You may also find an excess period that will apply to each claim. If your excess is 60 days and you claim for 70, then you will be paid for 10 days.

. . . and Maybe Your Credit Card

You may be one of those financially agile people
who are making maximum use of credit card balance
transfers (see credit card chapter). In that case, you may
have run up a significant credit card debt and want to
make sure that it is covered if something goes wrong.

Insurance companies offer you payment protection, and
it pays to shop around. When you take out a new credit
card you will probably be offered protection against
accident and sickness, unemployment or death (likely
to be run by an insurer). You need to compare costs and
examine the exclusions: in general, the policy will not
pay out for a pre-existing condition or if you knew – or
maybe should have known – that you were likely to be
made redundant.

Cutting Your Bills

There is a theory that saving money does not involve
a few major strategic moves but making a series of
individually small sensible decisions. The truth is that
you can, and should, do both: to make these small
sensible decisions you need to focus on your regular
outgoings – gas and electricity, insurance, telephones
and internet. Here are some ideas how you can save in
these areas:

Energy Switching
There is one essential step – you should compare
suppliers using an internet website. To make this

work, you need to know how much energy you use, which comes in kilowatt hours (kWh) for electricity. This information should appear on your energy bill. Otherwise, you can ask your supplier or just enter your existing supplier plus your typical spend and the site will probably be able to work out your consumption.

Using a comparison website matters, because it is estimated that one in three of all people who have changed their electricity supplier ended up with a more expensive tariff – which is a tribute to the complexity of energy tariffs. At the other extreme, ten million households – many of them pensioners – have never switched and could be paying more than they need.

Paperless is Cheaper
You will often find that 'dual-fuel' tariffs offer better value, where gas and electricity are billed together. You can make further savings by using a direct debit through your bank and maybe more by setting up online or paperless billing.

You need to check your market choice about once a year to make sure that you are still getting the most cost-effective deal. Like suppliers in many sectors, the utility companies may offer their best prices for new deals and push up the rates on older tariffs. Take care if you are contacted by telephone salesmen offering fuel deals: they are likely to represent individual suppliers and will not compare the whole market.

Insurance

A basic rule: when you get the papers to renew your home or car insurance, check round to see if you can get a better deal. You will probably need to use both the internet and the telephone, especially for car insurance. There are now a number of useful online insurance brokers.

Once you have decided whose policy to buy, it often makes sense to do the purchase online, where a number of insurers will offer you a discount. Another way to get a discount is to check if the company will accept monthly payments – and not, repeat not, charge you extra. Most companies will allow you to pay monthly, but many of these – not all – will charge you for the facility. This is your chance for an interest-free loan, so take it; and pay the premiums through your best cashback credit card.

Don't Let Someone Steal You!

Thousands of people have had their identity stolen – a modern, nasty piece of villainy, which you need to avoid. A thief steals your identity when he finds out your personal details and uses these data to open bank accounts, get credit cards and passports. If this happens, you may have problems with your bank and over your mortgage and credit cards. Getting this sorted out will take time and trouble.

▶

Remember: a great deal about you is already likely to be public knowledge – your full name, address and telephone number, your date and place of birth, the date and place of your marriage, your mother's maiden name, so do not make it any easier for the villains.

Some Danger Signs

Items you do not recognise appear on your bank or credit card statement.

You receive bills or receipts for goods you know nothing about.

Expected post does not arrive – such as your bank sending you a new cheque book.

You are turned down for a credit card though you have a good credit history.

How to Protect Yourself

Get a copy of your personal credit file every three or six months – it costs £2 from one of the credit reference agencies and is well worth it. If you move house, get a credit report a few months later.

Read your bank and credit card statements with care as soon as you get them.

Do not give out your personal details over the internet and only pay by credit card if there is evidence that the site is secure.

Take especial care when you use a PC that is not your own, say at an internet cafe.

If you lose a credit card, or if you think it's stolen, tell the company at once.

Be Prepared

Buy a shredder or a large pair of scissors to chop up credit card bills and bank statements – take care with unwanted post as this could also contain some of your personal details.

Keep important documents in a safe place, locked up or with your bank.

When your credit and debit cards expire, chop them up.

In choosing passwords, avoid family names or dates which an outsider could discover.

On your PC, use a firewall and anti-virus software: you may not always be able to stop someone stealing from you, but you do need to make it more difficult.

Travel insurance provides an area of great contrasts, where charges vary widely: most people now realise that buying travel insurance from a travel agent is not the most cost-effective, and use the internet, which they also accessed to buy their holiday. Two further savings are worth bearing in mind: one is to buy an annual policy, rather than take single-trip cover, if you or your family are regular travellers. According to one industry estimate, more than 5 million people are paying more than they need.

The second possible saving is to check out a bank account or a credit card that offers you free or low-cost travel insurance. You may have to top-up the cover which you are offered but the overall cost may still be less than buying direct. The bank account may be one for which you pay a fee, while credit cards are likely to offer you cover if you pay for your travel though them.

Telephone Bills . . .

Industry sources suggest that the average user could cut their mobile and landline bills by several hundred pounds a year by changing tariffs. Like gas and electricity users a few years ago, the majority of mobile users have never changed their supplier.

Your first stop, as with gas and electricity, is to use a comparison website. You then need to check your contract, to make sure that you are free to move. If you can move, look on the internet as well as for offers on the high street.

You may also be one of the many users who go above their monthly call and text allowances. This will cost you, as you will then be charged the standard rates. So you need to check your usage as it appears on your bills: you may need to change your tariff, maybe pay more to cut your total spend.

. . . with Broadband

You are very likely to want broadband, which is where your choices start to get complicated. There are reckoned to be around 100 providers of broadband, and many of the larger suppliers will offer you a package – broadband, telephone and TV bundled together.

To sort out the best for youself, you need first to decide what type of user you are going to be: light, medium or heavy. Then you need to access an online comparison site and make sure that you take on board any installation charges and what it costs to change your mind.

Price is important, but in this area service matters. Now, you can access customer satisfaction surveys, which are a useful guide – and which you need to repeat every six or 12 months.

Glossary

Terms Used In Finance

Annual Equivalent Rate (AER)   this shows what
the gross interest would be if interest were paid and
compounded on an annual basis.

Asset allocation   the way in which your money
is spread across a variety of markets, funds and
sectors. An important element in good investment
performance.

Basis points   City jargon relating to interest rates,
where 100 basis points equals 1%.

Bear market   when share prices are falling and
expected to keep on falling.

Bid/Offer Spread   in a unit trust, managers will buy
from you at the bid price and sell to you at the offer
price, generally about 5% higher.

Book value   the amount at which assets and
liabilities are reported in a company's financial
statement.

Bull market   when share prices are rising and

expected to keep on rising.

Derivatives   assets whose value derives from other assets – such as options and warrants.

Earnings per Share   After-tax profits attributable to ordinary shareholders divided by the number of shares outstanding.

Effective Annual Rate (EAR)   this is the rate, often on an overdraft, which takes into account how frequently interest is charged.

Emerging markets   stock markets in countries such as Brazil, China, India and Russia where the economies are growing fast – volatile and risky, but potentially profitable.

Futures contract   an agreement to buy or sell an asset, e.g. the value of a share index, on a fixed future date at a price agreed when the contract is taken out.

Gift with Reservation   gifts which you make but from which you continue to benefit, so they are treated as part of your estate for IHT.

Inflation   the Bank of England's official duty is to ensure that inflation does not breach the target of 2% by more than one percentage point. *Also see* Monetary Policy Committee.

Intestate   dying without a will, so your assets will be allocated under the intestacy rules. These rules are different in Scotland from England and Wales.

Joint tenants   typically, when a couple own a house, when one dies their share passes automatically to the survivor. *Also see* Tenants in Common.

LIBOR   The London Interbank Offered Rate, the interest rate charged by one bank to another for lending money.

Monetary Policy Committee   Bank of England nine-member group, created in 1997, to fix base rate, which determines short-term interest rates. *Also see* Inflation.

Net Asset Value (NAV)   the amount of the total equity divided by the number of ordinary shares in issue.

Nil Rate Band   the amount you can leave in your estate without paying IHT; fixed at £312,000 for 2008–9 – above that you pay 40%.

Open-Ended Investment Companies (OEICs)   modern development of unit trusts, which have one unit price – as opposed to bid/offer – and no trustee.

Option   an agreement which gives the right, but not the obligation, to buy or sell an asset at an agreed price on or before a fixed date.

Potentially Exempt Transfer   a gift you make, which will be free from IHT provided you survive for seven years – there will be IHT to pay, but on a reduced scale, if you survive for at least three years.

Pound Cost Averaging if you make regular payments, e.g. into a unit trust, the cost will average over a period as the price rises and falls – rather than putting in a lump sum at one time.

Real Estate Investment Trust (REIT) a public company with at least 75% of its profits and assets coming from property rental business. Income and capital gains are tax-free, but the REIT has to pay out a minimum 90% of its profits.

Return on Capital Employed Pre-interest profits divided by average capital employed – defined as shareholders' funds plus net debt.

Tenants in Common typically, when a couple own a house, when one dies their share passes as is specified in their will. *Also see* Joint Tenants.

Total Shareholder Return growth in value of a shareholding, assuming that dividends are ploughed back.

Unit trusts open-ended pooled funds where you can buy and sell units, whose price reflects the value of the underlying assets.

Zombie fund an investment plan, often a pension fund, which is closed to new customers.

Index